Newmarket Trainers' Directory 2013

Produced and Published by:
Thoroughbred Printing & Publishing
Hundon, Suffolk
e-mail: captiva@btinternet.com

List of horses courtesy of Weatherbys

Every effort has been made to ensure the accuracy of the information contained in this book at the time of going to press (15 June 2013).

NORCROFT FENCING:

Now "Covering" the UK, Ireland and the rest of Europe

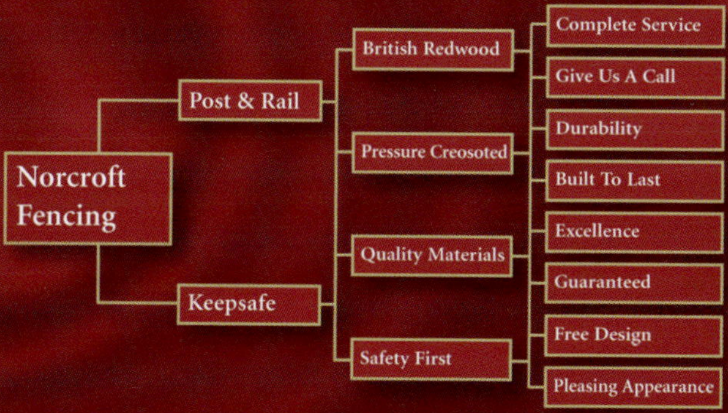

Contact Norcroft now to discuss the plans to construct, modernise or refurbish your stud or existing paddocks and see first hand why countless satisfied customers recommend you turn to Norcroft.

NORCROFT

Paddock Fencing

CONTACT RICHARD S JERMY ◆ NORCROFT EQUESTRIAN DEVELOPMENTS

1 Norton Road, Loddon, Norwich, Norfolk NR14 6JN Great Britain
Tel: 01508 520 743 ◆ Fax: 01508 528 879 ◆ Email: enquiries@norcroft.com

www.norcroft.com

NEWMARKET TRAINERS' FEDERATION

Chairman: Mark H Tompkins **Vice-Chairman:**William Jarvis

Introduction by Mark Tompkins

Once again the year seems to have flown by.

We are very lucky here in Newmarket, and really appreciate the fact, that we are supported by the biggest owners in the world. Our horse numbers have held up remarkably well, despite all the financial problems, and it is purely due to the overseas owners who seem to be recession-proof. Our British owners are struggling to balance the books and consequently are pulling in their horns as far as horse ownership is concerned. The news that Juddmonte Farms are to reduce their involvement has come as a bit of a shock to many people, but with the new investment from Qatar it might not have as great an impact as it could have done.

I would like to thank Nick Patton and his team on the heath who keep the gallops in tremendous order and are constantly upgrading and maintaining. It is still fantastic value to use the heath and there is no better place in the world to train.

We have recently been greatly saddened by the death of Sir Henry Cecil who fought cancer unbelievably bravely. He was the trainer every one of us looked up to and will be a great loss to the world of racing.

I would like to comment on the fixture list which, I have to say, is a complete mess. No effort has been made to improve it. It is already out for 2014 and I just hope somebody with an understanding of the industry can get it sorted out from 2015 onwards. The finances of the industry have still not been tackled properly and with the increase in phone and tablet betting more revenue goes to the offshore bookmakers. It must be impressed on the Government, and quickly, that this loss to the levy must be addressed. The betting shops, and we have at least 14 in Newmarket, are just becoming gaming machine arcades and is another avenue the government should attend to.

That's enough of my gripes. It just leaves me to say good luck to every Newmarket trainer for the rest of the year. May they continue to send out many more winners.

ROSSDALES UNVEILS NEW SCINTIGRAPHY SUITE AND IRIDIUM-192 THERAPY ROOM

Rossdales Equine Diagnostic Centre is pleased to announce the completion of our new scintigraphy (bone scan) suite and a new iridium (brachytherapy) room.

Rossdales has provided an equine scintigraphy service for more than 20 years. To keep in line with the advancement in all areas of equine diagnostic imaging, we made it one of our priorities for 2013 to update our facilities for this essential and busy service. As a practice, our ongoing commitment to investing in the latest equipment ensures that we continue to offer diagnostic and therapeutic services that are second to none.

Our brand new scintigraphy room, complete with state-of-the-art gamma camera, replaces our existing facility. The newly installed Equine Scanner HR Scintron® is the most advanced system available for equine scintigraphy, the only one of its kind in Newmarket and one of only three in the UK. It offers real advantages over other systems including an increased field of view and state-of-the-art motion correction software, which results in improved resolution and sharper contours of structures, extremely useful in areas such as the joints of the lower limb and complicated anatomic areas such as the teeth and spine.

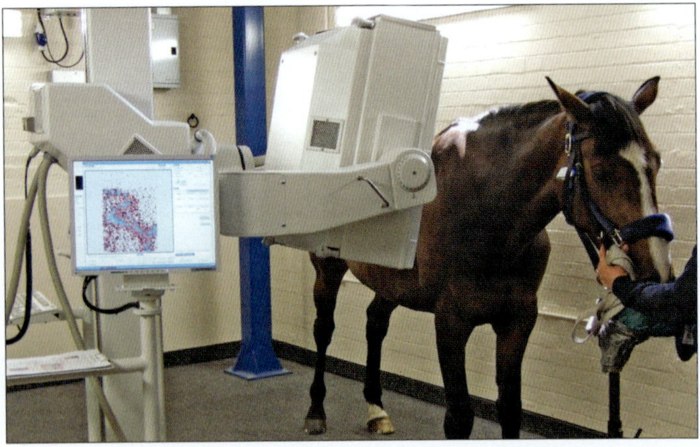

A horse undergoing a bone scan in the new scintigraphy suite

For the past two years, we have been offering iridium-192 therapy (brachytherapy) as a highly successful treatment for sarcoids and other tumours and we now have a dedicated facility for this purpose. Iridium-192 therapy is especially useful for the treatment of tumours that are in difficult locations (such as around the eye or over joints), or that have recurred despite other treatments. The treatment involves the insertion of small radioactive seeds directly into the tumour using sedation and local anaesthesia. The seeds are then left in place for a set period of time, usually 4-7 days, during which time they emit radiation directly into the area to kill the abnormal cells. At the end of the treatment, the seeds are removed and there is no residual radiation left in the horse. The success rate following treatment is usually 80-100%.

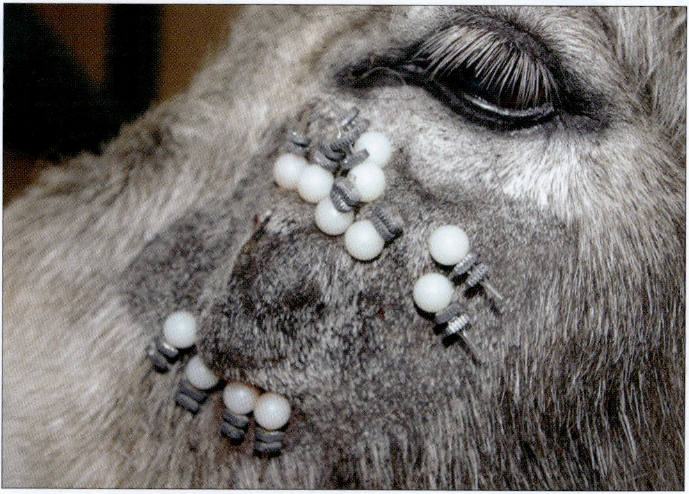

Iridium-192 therapy can be used successfully to treat sarcoids and other tumours

To refer a horse or pony for a bone scan, please contact Rossdales Equine Diagnostic Centre on 01638 577754.

If you have any specific questions about Iridium-192 therapy or would like to refer a horse or pony for treatment, please contact Emily Haggett at Rossdales Equine Hospital, either by email to emily.haggett@rossdales.com, or on 01638 577754.

ROSSDALES
VETERINARY SURGEONS

TRM
What do the top vendors in the UK, Ireland and the USA all have in common?
They choose Calphormin to ensure success.
UK Highclere Stud - Raised and consigned Derby Winner Camelot.
IRELAND Jim Bolger - Redmondstown Stud.
USA Ian Brennan - Pre-trainer of superstar broodmare Havre de Grace and Eddie Woods - Leading US Consigner, represented by 11 horses in the Breeders Cup races 2012.
CALPHORMIN
Available from: Farm and Stable Supplies LLP
Tel: +44 1730 815 800 Web: www.trm-store.co.uk
Manufactured in Ireland by: TRM
Newbridge Industrial Estate, Co. Kildare, Ireland
Tel: +353 45 434 358 Web: www.trm-ireland.com
Follow us on @TRMNutrition
CALPHORMIN
FOR OPTIMUM SKELETAL DEVELOPMENT & CONFORMATION

Clipper
15

Tattersalls

BY APPOINTMENT TO
HER MAJESTY THE QUEEN
SUPPLIERS OF SADDLERY CARE PRODUCTS
CARR & DAY & MARTIN LTD, LYTHAM

CARR & DAY & MARTIN®

OUR HISTORY

Carr & Day & Martin is the UK's oldest company involved in the manufacture of horse care products. Founded in 1765 we have Held a Royal Warrant since the reign of King George IV and still hold the Royal Warrant for the supply of quality saddlery care products to Her Majesty Queen Elizabeth II. We are dedicated to producing premium products that provide a complete care program for our discerning customers.

In September 2006, the company was acquired by the Tangerine Group of companies, a family business based in Lytham, Lancashire. Unlike many companies today, we actually manufacture our own products in our own factory. Quality is something we are fanatical about. Although there are no specific manufacturing requirements or standards laid down for manufacture of horse care products, we have for many years manufactured to pharmaceutical standards. We only use the highest specification ingredients, at optimum levels to deliver real results. This ensures our customers can have complete peace of mind when using our products.

Horse owners worldwide demand efficacy and value for money, and this is why over the last 248 years we have remained at the forefront of the equine industry. We recognise the need for continuous research and development and the associated investment in technology, and as a company that actually manufactures its own products, we are in an ideal position to drive and control this development.

We are committed to five core values –

Super premium products

Continuous investment in research and development

World class service

Long term partnerships

Industry leading education.

Remaining true to these values will ensure we continue to remain the leader in our field.

OUR PRODUCTS

The comprehensive range encompasses four distinct care categories: Leather, Coat, Hoof and Health Care, which provide a 'one-stop shop' for the discerning horse owner. Our Iconic brands that equine enthusiasts would know by name include Belvoir Leather Care, Gallop Shampoos, Vanner & Prest Hoof Care, Canter Coat Care and many more.

Horse Care has come a long way since our early days but we are proud to say that products such as our **Cornucrescine Original Hoof Ointment** have really stood the test of time, having been used and trusted since 1896. Quite an achievement we think.

This being said we never underestimate the importance of new, our heritage care products stand proudly alongside formulations based on the most up to date scientific research. Our **Cornucrescine Daily Hoof Barrier** for example, is ideal for preventing problems the modern horse owner faces. The advanced formulation uses technological advancements to waterproof the hoof, whilst still maintaining breathability and allowing the hoof to expel excess moisture. At Carr & Day & Martin we do not follow the latest fad or fashion and never will, as product innovation and efficacy is what sets us apart from the imitators.

For product advice or to find your nearest stockist please call our advice line on 0845 5004040 or visit our website at www.carrdaymartin.co.uk .

Hoof Care

Leather Care

Coat Care

Health Care

ALLSCAPE
Specialists in fencing and landscaping
Equestrian (post and rail / Tornado/ Keepsafe)
Agricultural (stock fencing / Rabbit fencing / barbed wire)
Domestic (closeboard / picket / Gates)
Security (palisade / gates)
Trenching / Water pipe installation
Paddock maintenance
Chemical weed control
Grass optimisation
Post and rail
Rabbit fencing
Chemical weed control
Domestic fences and gates
For more information
Please call (mobiles)
Justin 07771 960942
William 07789 934200
Or our office
01284 828714

New to the market from TRM - GNF Paste

Gastric disturbances are a major concern to the trainers, breeders, and owners of all performance horses. One such disturbance, Equine Gastric Ulcer Syndrome (EGUS), has become more prominent in recent years, with up to 93% of racehorses found to have ulcers on endoscopic examination.

In addition to the highly successful GNF Pellets, TRM introduced GNF Paste to the market earlier this year. GNF Paste is a complementary feedingstuff which is suitable for feeding to horses suffering from gastric disturbances, exhibiting as depressed appetite, weight loss, poor performance or cribbing.

GNF Pellets, when fed as a nutritional adjunct, has been shown, in major clinical trials presented at the World Equine Veterinary Association Congress, to reduce the incidence of gastric disturbances. GNF Paste is composed of all the key ingredients found in GNF Pellets, with the addition of Slippery Elm which is a natural source of mucilage. When fed at the recommended rate it will assist in the nutritional maintenance of a healthy digestive tract.

Tom Barrett, the TRM Vice President, sees GNF Paste as a natural extension to the product range, "Trainers and breeders all over the world are really convinced by the remarkable results achieved when feeding GNF. They have commented that their horses have a better appetite, fewer stable vices, hold their weight better and there is a general improvement in condition and performance. However customer feedback made it obvious to us that if horses are not eating well, it is difficult to ensure that the complementary feedingstuff is being ingested. With GNF Paste, Horse owners and trainers can ensure that the beneficial nutrients in the product are reaching their target, and once normal appetite has resumed the GNF Pellet is a more practical and affordable way to supplement. The paste is also very convenient for horses in transit."

In addition as a foal's stomach lining is thinner than that of the adult horse it is particularly susceptible to damage and thus EGUS has been reported as a common condition found in foals and yearlings. GNF Paste is effective when used to stabilise the intestinal microflora in newborn foals. It acts as a gut conditioner by controlling pH and reducing the impact of stress and diet changes. The inclusion of slippery elm results in a significant improvement in the quantity of quality of mucilage in the stomach, and is a significant advancement in the product range. GNF Paste is an easily assimilated food for young and geriatric animals.

For more information on GNF Paste contact Farm and Stable Supplies on + 44 1730 815 800.

Dansili

DAY, SON AND HEWITT

Day, Son and Hewitt have been established since 1833, founded in London their first product on the marketplace was the black drench an innovative product which was a brilliant support to colic sufferer's and saved many horses lives. In 1865 they were awarded the Royal Warrant for Veterinary products which nearly 150 years on they still hold today.

Manufacturing in the 1900's moved North, Bradford then to Lancaster and still remains in the North West today in Lytham in Lancashire.

Day, Son and Hewitt today manufacture nutraceutical's using the latest research and development with equine nutritional expertise to provide a super-premium range which address's 80% of environmental issues used by breeders, professionals and horse owners alike.

The range of seven products supports, Joints, Hooves, Energy, Wellbeing, Performance, Calming, Ulcers, Colic, Laminitis, Poor Digestive Health and are FEI compliant.

Packed in individual daily sachets keep active ingredients, including fat and water soluble vitamins fresh for ultimate efficacy and accurate uncontaminated dosing.

Synoflex for Joints and inflammation

Is a leading joint product in the marketplace, with optimum levels of Chondroitin Sulphate, Glucosamine Hydrochloride, MSM, Vitamin C and Manganese , increases the production of Proteoglycans and Collagen ensuring young professional horses have the ultimate protection for their joints supporting soundness and anti-inflammatory for vital performance. Synoflex is a very effective natural alternative to phenylbutazone

Synoflex is available online at daysonhewitt.co.uk with free UK next day delivery. A month's supply contains 30 sachets to be administrated daily. RRp £69.00

For further information on the range please contact our advice line on

08455007777

www.daysonhewitt.co.uk

RACING'S SILENT WEAPON - DHA RICH OILS

Oils are a great source of energy but it's extremely important that trainers know the difference between an oil high in omega 6 and one rich in omega 3/DHA.

Then if you look further into this, there is a 10 fold difference in the effectiveness of short chain versus long chain omega 3's. The latter has some serious health and performance benefits that will affect your team directly, read on to find out more...

The Power of Long Chain Omega 3

Results from ongoing studies around the world have provided a wealth of evidence to show how omega 3 fatty acids alter biochemical and molecular processes. The data shows consistent and reproducible beneficial effects for man and animals of omega-3 fatty acids on bone metabolism, bone/joint diseases, gene expression, immuno-competence and disease resistance. Omega 3 fatty acids therefore have a central role to play in maintaining health and also in the management and prevention of many 'modern' diseases.

Omega 3 oils alter cell wall flexibility, support immune function, control the body's response to inflammation and provide an additional source of anti-oxidants. When omega 3 oils are returned to the diet, a reduction in cholesterol, clotting abnormalities and blood pressure have been reported in clinical studies in animals and in man. Other studies highlight the importance of Omega 3 fatty acids in reducing pain and inflammation in human patients with degenerative joint disease, rheumatoid arthritis, and osteo-arthritis. Omega 3 oils provide an important

source of omega 3 fatty acids. Fatty acids form a crucial role in the body, being part of the lipid bi-layer in cell membranes throughout the body.

The relative amounts of omega 3 and omega 6 fatty acids found in these cell membranes has been shown to be influenced by their relative abundance in the diet.

As the Omega 3 content of the diet increases, so does the structural content of cell membranes, which helps mediate their positive physiological effects. Importantly for performance or competition horses, omega 3 oils have been shown to have an impact on the membrane structure of red blood cell walls –increasing their flexibility and fluidity. This is an advantage during exercise as the cells can pass more easily through the narrow capillaries in the lungs and muscles, making oxygen uptake and delivery as well as waste product removal, more efficient. This may also help to reduce pressure in the fine capillaries of the lungs, reducing the chance of exercise-induced haemorrhage (bleeding). Human athletes with omega 3-supplemented diets report improved performance and less delayed muscle soreness with this being attributed to improved oxygen delivery, and anti-oxidant status in association with the protective affect omega 3 oils have against inflammation.

Sub optimal dietary intake of micronutrients such as zinc, biotin and methionine are well known to contribute to poor hoof quality. It may be less widely known that omega 3 fatty acids also have an important role to play and an insufficient dietary omega 3 intake has been linked to hoof defects such as shelly feet. Whilst other nutrients can be easily provided through the normal concentrate feed, omega-3 oil needs to be specifically supplemented.

Vegetable oils, such as corn and soybean oil, contain a high level of omega 6 fatty acids, which will ultimately be converted into longer chain omega 6 fatty acids in direct competition with the formation of analogous omega 3 fatty acids.

Corn and soya oil will therefore favour the incorporation of these omega 6 fatty acids into cell membranes throughout the body, at the expense of comparable omega-3 fatty acids. This may have a negative impact on some physiological processes.

The tissues of wild horses contain relatively higher amounts of omega-3 fatty acids compared to domesticated horses. So where have the omega-3 fatty acids gone? Domestication brought a change in diet including reduced

grazing, increased use of conserved forage as well as increased consumption of grains, and omega 6 rich oils e.g. corn and sunflower oils. These modern equine diets are in general higher in omega-6 fatty acids and access to good grass, which is a reasonable source of omega 3 fatty acids, is often severely reduced.

Today's horse diets contain very few direct dietary sources of DHA, and so it must be synthesised from a building block present in the diet in the form of -linolenic acid. Whilst flax or linseed oil is a rich source of -linolenic acid and will be of some benefit, unfortunately the conversion of -linolenic acid to either EPA or DHA is a very slow and inefficient process. It is much more efficient therefore to provide a supplementary direct source of EPA and DHA in the diet.

A Keyflow® Approach to Feeding Omega 3

To get the maximum benefit of short chain and direct source long chain omega 3/DHA, top dress your horses feed with Keyflow® Key-3 Oil. This blended equine specific oil is an ideal supplementary source of -linolenic acid, but more importantly of DHA and EPA.

With bulk rates available to yards, feeding Key-3 Oil can start from as little as 35p per horse, per day at full dose rates.

For further information on Keyflow® super-premium feeds and specialist supplements phone +44 (0)1672 51 9000, email advice@keyflowfeeds.com or visit www.keyflowfeeds.com

IMMUNALL

NATURAL FOOD SUPPLEMENTS

Immunall LTD, head office and manufacturing facility
Heathlands Farm, Ashwicken Rd, East Winch, King's Lynn, Norfolk, PE32 1LJ
Tel: + 44 (0) 1553 630 699 E-mail: brandes@immunall.com Website:www.immunall.com

IMMUNALL

is a nutritional supplement that supports the horse's immune system by helping to cleanse the body from a build-up of unwanted toxins. The patented combination contains extracts of Allium sativum, Uncaria tomentosa, Eleutherococcus scenticosus, Echinacea purpurea, Juglans regia, Carduus marianus and Viola tricolor to help keep your horse looking, feeling and performing at its very best.
Immunall is suitable for use in any animal, from a high-performance sports horse to a pony in light work The powerful combination of natural herbs provides visible results within days, and helps keep a horse's energy levels at their maximum.
We believe stress is one of the major risk factors to a horse's health. Whether that stress is biological as a result of an infection, mental as a result of the surrounding environment or physical due to the way we ask a horse to exert itself, the results are the same. Stress triggers a chemical reaction within the body that can lead to a poorly functioning immune system and internal organs.
Often the signs are so subtle we completely miss them. Immunall may be useful in a variety of different capacities within the horse world.

Breeding

Viruses, bacteria and fungi, along with hormonal problems and host of other diseases, can have devastating effects on fertility in both mares and stallions and on the unborn foal.

Competition

Even at a low level, competition places unusual stress on a horse: travelling to an event, mixing with other equines (which may be carrying disease) and the physical exertion involved. Added to this, depleted energy levels and high levels of toxic waste in the body post-competition can leave a horse open to infection.

Racing

Racehorses are asked to perform at their maximum output on a regular basis, and their environment and feeding pattern is very strictly controlled. Horses often travel vast distances to races, mixing with others from all over the country. During such a high-stress environment, particularly after a race, the horse is more vulnerable to disease, increasing the risk of cross-contamination.

General maintenance

In their natural environment, horses and ponies move around most of the day and night while foraging for food. This keeps their joints and bodily systems supple and working correctly. When we stable a horse, it is forced to be stationary for long periods of time.

WHAT USERS ARE SAYING .....

Juliet Minton, horse breeder "We use it on everything, the foals and broodmares, for sales preparation and our point-to-pointers. We've been using it for about 18 months and it definitely helps to keep the horses healthier."
Ed Dunlop, racehorse trainer "We've been delighted with the results from using Immunall, the horses have certainly seemed a lot healthier since we've been using the product."
Mrs Jessica Harrington, racehorse trainer "I am delighted with the results of Immunall and find it very effective on horses that run below par."

One of Britain's largest privately-owned horse transport fleets
NRT
NEWMARKET (RACEHORSE) TRANSPORT INTERNATIONAL
NRT
Offering a totally comprehensive Horse Transport service, including domestic and international shipments
Office address:
Cricket Field Road
Newmarket
Suffolk CB8 8BT
IVECO
Tel: 01638 663155
Fax: 01638 560894
HT12 NRT
Mobile: 07776 208503
Email: info@nrt-international.com

TRAINERS IN THE NEWMARKET AREA 2013

Conrad Allen

Saffron House Stables, Hamilton Road, Newmarket, CB8 0NY
Correspondence to Byerley House, Warrington Street, Newmarket CB8 8BA

Tel: 01638 666660 01638667870 (h) **Mobile:** 07802 692621 **Fax:** 01638 668005

3 YEAR OLDS

001 **AFORTUNADO** (IRE) 3 b c Footstepsinthesand - Bon Expresso (IRE) (Spectrum (IRE))
002 **AZMA** (USA) 3 b f Bernardini (USA) - Dyna's Destiny (USA) (Dynaformer (USA))
003 **GRIVOLA** (GER) 3 b f Ransom O'War (USA) - Ginza (GER) (Acatenango (GER))
004 **ROUGE NUAGE** (IRE) 3 ch g Indian Haven - Nom Francais (First Trump)

2 YEAR OLDS

005 **ARTEMIS** (IRE) 2 b f Marju (IRE) - Silver Arrow (USA) (Shadeed (USA))
006 **CHARLIE'S WISH** (FR) 2 b f Myboycharlie (IRE) - Lindsey's Wish (USA) (Trippi (USA))
007 **IRISH PURSUITS** (GER) 2 b c Pastoral Pursuits - Irish Eagle (GER) (Eagle Eyed (USA))
008 **TEMPELFEUER** (GER) 2 b f Soldier Hollow - Tempelsonne (GER) (Acatenango (GER))
009 unnamed 2 b c Soldier Hollow - Sunshine Story (IRE) (Desert Story (IRE))

Alan Bailey

Cavendish Stables, Hamilton Road, Newmarket, Suffolk, CB8 7JQ

Tel: 01638 664546 **Mobile:** 07808 734223

OLDER HORSES

001 **BUBBLY BALLERINA** 4 ch f Footstepsinthesand - Pain Perdu (IRE) (Waajib)
002 **DAZZLING VALENTINE** 5 b m Oratorio (IRE) - Bedazzling (IRE) (Darshaan)
003 **OUTPOST** (IRE) 5 ch g Giant's Causeway (USA) - Southern Migration (USA) (Kingmambo (USA))
004 **SON VIDA** (IRE) 5 b g Titus Livius (FR) - Sombreffe (Polish Precedent (USA))
005 **ST IGNATIUS** 6 b g Ishiguru (USA) - Branston Berry (IRE) (Mukaddamah (USA))
006 **STRICTLY SILVER** (IRE) 4 gr g Dalakhani (IRE) - Miss Chaussini (IRE) (Rossini (USA))

3 YEAR OLDS

007 **BADDILINI** 3 b g Bertolini (USA) - Baddi Heights (FR) (Shirley Heights)
008 **COINCIDENTLY** 3 b f Acclamation - Miss Chaussini (IRE) (Rossini (USA))
009 **EQUITANIA** 3 b f Pastoral Pursuits - Clarice Orsini (Common Grounds)
010 **GO FAR** 3 b g Dutch Art - Carranita (IRE) (Anita's Prince)
011 **KING GEORGE RIVER** (IRE) 3 b c Danehill Dancer (IRE) - Butterfly Blue (IRE) (Sadler's Wells (USA))
012 **MEGALEKA** 3 b f Misu Bond (IRE) - Peyto Princess (Bold Arrangement)
013 **SIXTIES QUEEN** 3 b f Sixties Icon - Lily of Tagula (IRE) (Tagula (IRE))

2 YEAR OLDS

014 **ANYTIMEATALL** (IRE) 2 b f Kodiac - Under My Skin (IRE) (Mark of Esteem (IRE))
015 **MIMI LUKE** (USA) 2 b f U S Ranger (USA) - Hard As Nails (USA) (Holy Bull (USA))
016 **SAFFIRE SONG** 2 ch f Firebreak - Saffwah (IRE) (King's Best (USA))
017 **TRINITY LORRAINE** (IRE) 2 b f Dark Angel (IRE) - Known Class (USA) (Known Fact (USA))

Michael Bell

Fitzroy House, Black Bear Lane, Newmarket CB8 0JT

Tel: 01638 666567 **Fax:** 01638 668000 **Mobile:** 07802 264514

OLDER HORSES

001 **ALLIED POWERS** (IRE) 8 b g Invincible Spirit (IRE) - Always Friendly (High Line)
002 **BITE OF THE CHERRY** 4 ro f Dalakhani (IRE) - Bianca Nera (Salse (USA))
003 **BORN TO SURPRISE** 4 b g Exceed And Excel (AUS) - Dubai Surprise (IRE) (King's Best (USA))
004 **CREME ANGLAISE** 5 b m Motivator - Reading Habit (USA) (Half a Year (USA))
005 **KING OF JAZZ** (IRE) 5 b g Acclamation - Grand Slam Maria (FR) (Anabaa (USA))
006 **ONE KOOL DUDE** 4 ch g Iceman - Hiraeth (Petong)
007 **REFRACTOR** (IRE) 5 ch g Refuse To Bend (IRE) - Fancy Intense (Peintre Celebre (USA))
008 **RUTLAND BOY** 5 ch g Bertolini (USA) - Israar (Machiavellian (USA))
009 **SIGN MANUAL** 4 b g Motivator - New Assembly (IRE) (Machiavellian (USA))
010 **SOVEREIGN DEBT** (IRE) 4 gr c Dark Angel (IRE) - Kelsey Rose (Most Welcome)
011 **SURAJ** 4 ch c Galileo (IRE) - Maid of Killeen (IRE) (Darshaan)
012 **THE BETCHWORTH** KID 8 b g Tobougg (IRE) - Runelia (Runnett)
013 **WIGMORE HALL** (IRE) 6 b g High Chaparral (IRE) - Love And Laughter (IRE) (Theatrical)

3 YEAR OLDS

014 **ALGORITHMIC** (IRE) 3 b g Danehill Dancer (IRE) - Tanami Desert (Lycius (USA))
015 **AZRUR** (IRE) 3 b g Sir Percy - Tiger Spice (Royal Applause)
016 **BILL OF RIGHTS** 3 b f Kyllachy - Bijou A Moi (Rainbow Quest (USA))
017 **CAPELLA'S SONG** (IRE) 3 b f Oratorio (IRE) - Bright Bank (IRE) (Sadler's Wells (USA))
018 **CHEBIKA** 3 b f Oasis Dream - Dancing Abbie (USA) (Theatrical)
019 **DALLIEFOUR** (IRE) 3 b f Cape Cross (IRE) - Daliyana (IRE) (Cadeaux Genereux)
020 **DEFICIT** (IRE) 3 gr c Dalakhani (IRE) - Venturi (Danehill Dancer (IRE))
021 **DIVERGENCE** (IRE) 3 b f Teofilo (IRE) - Min Alhawa (USA) (Riverman (USA))
022 **FANNY SQUEERS** 3 b f New Approach (IRE) - Whazzat (Daylami (IRE))
023 **FASHION** LINE (IRE) 3 b f Cape Cross (IRE) - Shadow Roll (IRE) (Mark of Esteem (IRE))
024 **FILS ANGES** (IRE) 3 gr c Dark Angel (IRE) - La Piaf (FR) (Fabulous Dancer (USA))
025 **FORCED FAMILY FUN** 3 b g Refuse To Bend (IRE) - Juniper Girl (IRE) (Revoque (IRE))
026 **GAMBLE** 3 ch f Galileo (IRE) - Pretty Face (Rainbow Quest (USA))
027 **GEORGE CINQ** 3 b c Pastoral Pursuits - Fairnilee (Selkirk (USA))
028 **HANDIWORK** 3 ch g Motivator - Spinning Top (Alzao (USA))
029 **HARTWRIGHT** 3 b g Exceed And Excel (AUS) - All For Laura (Cadeaux Genereux)
030 **HISPANIA** (IRE) 3 b f Teofilo (IRE) - Badalona (Cape Cross (IRE))
031 **HOT MUSTARD** 3 b g Pastoral Pursuits - Lihou Island (Beveled (USA))
032 **HOYAM** 3 b f Royal Applause - Christmas Tart (IRE) (Danetime (IRE))
033 **HUNTSMANS CLOSE** 3 b g Elusive Quality (USA) - Badminton (Zieten (USA))
034 **JADESNUMBERONE** (IRE) 3 b f Authorized (IRE) - Gabriella (Cape Cross (IRE))
035 **KENSINGTON GARDENS** 3 b f Oasis Dream - Wendylina (IRE) (In The Wings)
036 **LOVESOME** 3 b f Kheleyf (USA) - Heavenly Bay (USA) (Rahy (USA))
037 **MADAME DEFARGE** (IRE) 3 b f Motivator - Friendlier (Zafonic (USA))
038 **MOVES LIKE JAGGER** (IRE) 3 b c Danehill Dancer (IRE) - Lucky Spin (Pivotal)
039 **MRS MICAWBER** 3 gr f Nayef (USA) - Under The Rainbow (Fantastic Light (USA))
040 OILINDA 3 b f Nayef (USA) - Loyal Love (USA) (Danzig (USA))
041 **PENANG POWER** 3 b f Manduro (GER) - Penang Pearl (FR) (Bering)
042 **POINT OF CONTROL** 3 b f Pivotal - Finlaggan (Be My Chief (USA))
043 **PRINCESS PATSKY** (USA) 3 b br f Mr Greeley (USA) - Kamarinskaya (USA) (Storm Cat (USA))
044 **RISKIT FORA BISKIT** (IRE) 3 b f Kodiac - Miss Brief (IRE) (Brief Truce (USA))
045 **SANTO PRINCE** (USA) 3 b br g Henrythenavigator (USA) - Sally Wood (CAN) (Woodman (USA))
046 **SHANTI** 3 b c Dansili - Maycocks Bay (Muhtarram (USA))

047 **SHREWD** 3 b g Street Sense (USA) - Cala (FR) (Desert Prince (IRE))
048 **SPIRITUAL GIRL** 3 gr f Invincible Spirit (IRE) - Clizia (IRE) (Machiavellian (USA))
049 **STAR OF ROHM** 3 ch g Exceed And Excel (AUS) - Noble Desert (FR) (Green Desert (USA))
050 **SUGAR COATED** (IRE) 3 b f Duke of Marmalade (IRE) - Crystal Curling (IRE) (Peintre Celebre (USA))
051 **THE LARK** 3 ch f Pivotal - Gull Wing (IRE) (In The Wings)
052 **THE MANX MISSILE** 3 ch g Sakhee's Secret - Careless Freedom (Bertolini (USA))
053 **WILDCRAFTING** 3 ch f Exceed And Excel (AUS) - Local Spirit (USA) (Lion Cavern (USA))
054 **WINSLOW ARIZONA** (IRE) 3 b g Danehill Dancer (IRE) - Buffalo Berry (IRE) (Sri Pekan (USA))
055 **ZERO GAME** (IRE) 3 b f High Chaparral (IRE) - Freezing Love (USA) (Danzig (USA))

2 YEAR OLDS

056 **AL KHAWANEEJ** STAR (USA) 2 b br c Arch (USA) - Frolic Away (USA) (Pentelicus (USA))
057 **ALMAX** 2 b c Rock of Gibraltar (IRE) - Inya Lake (Whittingham (IRE))
058 **BORN TO REIGN** 2 b c Sir Percy - Oat Cuisine (Mujahid (USA))
059 **CHATHAM HOUSE RULE** 2 gr c Authorized (IRE) - Cozy Maria (USA) (Cozzene (USA))
060 EXCEEDING POWER 2 b c Exceed And Excel (AUS) - Extreme Beauty (USA) (Rahy (USA))
061 **FINN CLASS** (IRE) 2 b c Exceed And Excel (AUS) - Finnmark (Halling (USA))
062 **FUTOON** 2 b f Royal Applause - Cefira (USA) (Distant View (USA))
063 **GALIZZI** (USA) 2 b c Dansili - Dancing Abbie (USA) (Theatrical)
064 **GENDER AGENDA** 2 b f Holy Roman Emperor (IRE) - Friendlier (Zafonic (USA))
065 **GOOD HOPE** 2 b f Cape Cross (IRE) - Fairy Godmother (Fairy King (USA))
066 **HALA HALA** (IRE) 2 b f Invincible Spirit (IRE) - Galistic (IRE) (Galileo (IRE))
067 **HAPPY CLAPPY** (IRE) 2 b c Art Connoisseur (IRE) - Narmeen (Royal Applause)
068 **INVOKE** (IRE) 2 b f Kodiac - Tides (Bahamian Bounty)
069 **MANTOU** (IRE) 2 ch c Teofilo (IRE) - Shadow Roll (IRE) (Mark of Esteem (IRE))
070 **NEWMARKET WARRIOR** (IRE) 2 b c Dalakhani (IRE) - Heavens Peak (Pivotal)
071 **PIAZON** 2 br c Striking Ambition - Colonel's Daughter (Colonel Collins (USA))
072 **RHONDA** (IRE) 2 b f Fastnet Rock (AUS) - Regal Darcey (IRE) (Darshaan)
073 **ROCK OF LEON** 2 b c Rock of Gibraltar (IRE) - Leonica (Lion Cavern (USA))
074 **SONG BEAM** 2 ch f Shamardal (USA) - Basanti (USA) (Galileo (IRE))
075 **SPEEDY APPROACH** 2 ch c New Approach (IRE) - Height of Vanity (IRE) (Erhaab (USA))
076 **SPIRITOFTHEUNION** 2 b f Authorized (IRE) - Kahlua Kiss (Mister Baileys)
077 **SUGAR RUSH** 2 ch c Pastoral Pursuits - Panic Stations (Singspiel (IRE))
078 **SUNNINGDALE ROSE** (IRE) 2 b f Art Connoisseur (IRE) - Eloquent Rose (IRE) (Elnadim (USA))
079 **TAUTIRA** (IRE) 2 b f Kheleyf (USA) - Ballantrae (IRE) (Diktat)
080 **THATCHEREEN** (IRE) 2 b f Mastercraftsman (IRE) - Roof Fiddle (USA) (Cat Thief (USA))
081 **VALEN** (IRE) 2 gr f Acclamation - Ardea Brave (IRE) (Chester House (USA))
082 **WADI ALAMARDI** 2 ch c Lucky Story (USA) - Thicket (Wolfhound (USA))
083 **WEDDING WISH** (IRE) 2 b f Acclamation - Have Faith (IRE) (Machiavellian (USA))
084 unnamed 2 b c Fastnet Rock (AUS) - Bowstring (IRE) (Sadler's Wells (USA))
085 unnamed 2 ch f Manduro (GER) - Cape Marien (IRE) (Cape Cross (IRE))
086 unnamed 2 ch gr c Aqlaam - Good Enough (FR) (Mukaddamah (USA))
087 unnamed 2 b c Street Cry (IRE) - Say No Now (IRE) (Refuse To Bend (IRE))
088 unnamed 2 gr c Mastercraftsman (IRE) - Wait It Out (USA) (Swain (IRE))

John Berry

Beverley House Stables, Exeter Road, Newmarket, Suffolk CB8 8LR

Tel & Fax: 01638 660663

OLDER HORSES

001 **ANNIA GALERIA** (IRE) 6 b m Antonius Pius (USA) - Jay Gee (IRE) (Second Set (IRE))
002 **DOUCHKIRK** (FR) 6 b g Prince Kirk (FR) - Douchka (FR) (Fijar Tango (FR))
003 **ETHICS GIRL** (IRE) 7 b m Hernando (FR) - Palinisa (FR) (Night Shift (USA))
004 **GIFT OF SILENCE** 4 gr f Cadeaux Genereux - Not A Word (Batshoof)
005 **GRAND LIAISON** 4 b f Sir Percy - Dancinginthedark (IRE) (Fasliyev (USA))
006 **SIMAYILL** 5 b m Oasis Dream - Triennial (IRE) (Giant's Causeway (USA))
007 **WASABI** (IRE) 4 b f Tiger Hill (IRE) - Quinzey (JPN) (Carnegie (IRE))
008 **ZAROSA** (IRE) 4 b f Barathea (IRE) - Shantalla Peak (IRE) (Darshaan)

3 YEAR OLDS

009 **ORLA'S RAINBOW** (IRE) 3 b c Oratorio (IRE) - Red Ray (Pivotal)
010 **PLATINUM PROOF** (USA) 3 b br c Smart Strike (CAN) - Keeper Hill (USA) (Deputy Minister (CAN))
011 **PURRFECT** 3 b f Tiger Hill (IRE) - B Beautiful (IRE) (Be My Guest (USA))
012 **ROY ROCKET** (FR) 3 gr g Layman (USA) - Minnie's Mystery (FR) (Highest Honor (FR))

2 YEAR OLDS

013 **INDIRA** 2 ch f Sleeping Indian - Forever Loved (Deploy)

GROSVENOR
PHYSIOTHERAPY CLINIC

"Take care of your body. It's the only place you have to live."
Jim Rohn

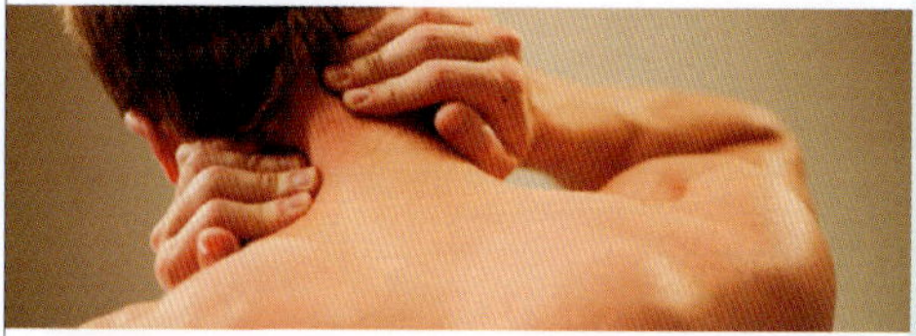

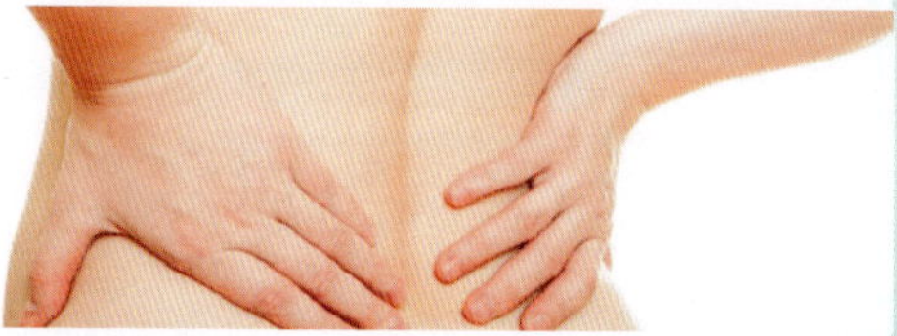

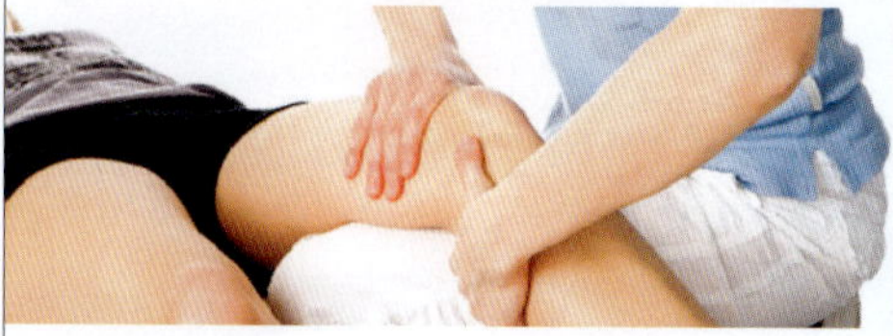

- Neck and Back Pain
- Sciatica, lumbago, "slipped disc" (prolapse)
- Whiplash
- Headaches
- Jaw pain
- Other spinal conditions
- Joint problems including arthritis
- Frozen shoulder
- Tennis or golfers elbow
- Ankle and foot problems such as plantar fasciitis, metatarsalgia
- Achilles tendon problems
- Knee pain
- Sports injuries
- Chronic pain
- Post surgical rehabilitation
- Muscle problems
- Muscle imbalance
- Postural problems
- Neurological disorders, for example recovery from head injury or stroke
- Chest conditions such as chronic bronchitis, bronchiectasis, emphysema, asthma
- Workplace injuries and problems
- Repetitive strain injury
- General aches and pains

Physiotherapy for your aches, pains and injuries

The Grosvenor Physiotherapy Clinic in Newmarket offers a wide range of treatments carried out by a team of experienced and fully qualified physiotherapists.
The Practice is registered with BUPA, AXAPPP, Aviva, WPA and most other medical insurance companies. To make an appointment please telephone 01638 667606.

Diana Hall Physiotherapy Ltd
Grosvenor Physiotherapy Clinic
154a High Street
Newmarket
CB8 9AQ

Telephone/Fax: 01638 667606

Physio First

hpc health professions council

Email: dianahallphysiotherapy@btconnect.com
www.grosvenorphysionewmarket.co.uk

Marco Botti

PRESTIGE PLACE STABLES, SNAILWELL ROAD, NEWMARKET, SUFFOLK CB8 7DP
ADDITIONAL YARD: GREEN RIDGE STABLES, HAMILTON ROAD, NEWMARKET CB8 7JQ

Tel: 01638 662416 **Fax:** 01638 662417 **Mobile:** 07775 803007

OLDER HORSES

001 **DANDINO** 6 br h Dansili - Generous Diana (Generous (IRE))
002 **DE RIGUEUR** 5 b g Montjeu (IRE) - Exclusive (Polar Falcon (USA))
003 **FATTSOTA** 5 b g Oasis Dream - Gift of The Night (USA) (Slewpy (USA))
004 **FOUR LEAVES** (IRE) 4 ch f Singspiel (IRE) - My Heart's Deelite (USA) (Afternoon Deelites (USA))
005 **GREY MIRAGE** 4 b g Oasis Dream - Grey Way (USA) (Cozzene (USA))
006 **GUEST OF HONOUR** (IRE) 4 b c Cape Cross (IRE) - Risera (IRE) (Royal Academy (USA))
007 **HALFSIN** (IRE) 5 b g Haafhd - Firesteed (IRE) (Common Grounds)
008 **HAMBLE** 4 b g Librettist (USA) - Time For Tea (IRE) (Imperial Frontier (USA))
009 **HEFNER** (IRE) 4 b g Tagula (IRE) - Classic Style (IRE) (Desert Style (IRE))
010 **MASAMAH** (IRE) 7 gr g Exceed And Excel (AUS) - Bethesda (Distant Relative)
011 **MEZZOTINT** (IRE) 4 b g Diamond Green (FR) - Aquatint (Dansili)
012 **MODERN ROMANCE** (IRE) 4 ch f Muhtathir - Khulan (USA) (Bahri (USA))
013 **PLANTEUR** (IRE) 6 b h Danehill Dancer (IRE) - Plante Rare (IRE) (Giant's Causeway (USA))
014 **PLEINE FORME** (USA) 5 b m Grand Slam (USA) - Why Worry (FR) (Cadeaux Genereux)
015 **SEACHANTACH** (USA) 7 b g Elusive Quality (USA) - Subtle Breeze (USA) (Storm Cat (USA))
016 **SHAMDARLEY** (IRE) 5 b g Shamardal (USA) - Siphon Melody (USA) (Siphon (BRZ))
017 **SOLAR DEITY** (IRE) 4 b c Exceed And Excel (AUS) - Dawn Raid (IRE) (Docksider (USA))
018 **SOUVIENS** TOI 4 b f Dalakhani (IRE) - Diavla (USA) (Bahri (USA))
019 **SPIFER** (IRE) 5 gr g Motivator - Zarawa (IRE) (Kahyasi)
020 **SUEGIOO** (FR) 4 ch c Manduro (GER) - Mantesera (IRE) (In The Wings)
021 **WHAILEYY** (IRE) 5 b g Holy Roman Emperor (IRE) - Alshoowg (USA) (Riverman (USA))

3 YEAR OLDS

022 **AL EMIRATI** (IRE) 3 b c Tamayuz - Corrine (IRE) (Spectrum (IRE))
023 **AL GHARRAFA** 3 b f Dutch Art - Smart Ass (IRE) (Shinko Forest (IRE))
024 **AL RAQEEB** (IRE) 3 b c Lawman (FR) - Caerlina (IRE) (Caerleon (USA))
025 **AUTSPREAD** 3 b c Authorized (IRE) - Ridotto (Salse (USA))
026 **AVATAR STAR** (IRE) 3 b g Peintre Celebre (USA) - Homegrown (IRE) (Mujadil (USA))
027 **BELLITUDO** (IRE) 3 ch f Shamardal (USA) - Night Life (IRE) (Night Shift (USA))
028 **BERN ME BABY** (USA) 3 b f Bernstein (USA) - Clever Maid (USA) (Confide (USA))
029 **CAMACHOICE** (IRE) 3 b g Camacho - Nouvelle Reve (GER) (Acatenango (GER))
030 **CENTURIUS** 3 ch c New Approach (IRE) - Questina (FR) (Rainbow Quest (USA))
031 **DUCHESS OF SEVILLE** 3 b f Duke of Marmalade (IRE) - Serrenia (IRE) (High Chaparral (IRE))
032 **FIRST SARGEANT** 3 gr c Dutch Art - Princess Raya (Act One)
033 **FORWARD** (IRE) 3 b c Danehill Dancer (IRE) - Drifting (IRE) (Sadler's Wells (USA))
034 **GIOIA DI VITA** 3 b c Sakhee (USA) - Dhuyoof (IRE) (Sinndar (IRE))
035 **GRENDISAR** (IRE) 3 b c Invincible Spirit (IRE) - Remarkable Story (Mark of Esteem (IRE))
036 **HASOPOP** (IRE) 3 b g Haatef (USA) - Convenience (IRE) (Ela-Mana-Mou)
037 **IZIL** 3 ch c Manduro (GER) - Junior Council (IRE) (Sadler's Wells (USA))
038 **KATTAF** (IRE) 3 ch c Hernando (FR) - Decision Maid (USA) (Diesis)
039 **MAGICAL KINGDOM** (IRE) 3 b c Danehill Dancer (IRE) - Al Saqiya (USA) (Woodman (USA))
040 **MAGIKA** 3 b f Dubawi (IRE) - Aline's Wings (ITY) (In The Wings)
041 **MAKIN** (IRE) 3 b c Shirocco (GER) - Cuca Vela (USA) (Devil's Bag (USA))
042 **MARCH** 3 b f Dutch Art - Royal Pardon (Royal Applause)
043 **MAUGHAMI** 3 b gr f Manduro (GER) - Grey Way (USA) (Cozzene (USA))
044 **MAXIMITO** 3 b c Motivator - Lorien Hill (IRE) (Danehill (USA))
045 **MESMERIZED** (IRE) 3 b f Duke of Marmalade (IRE) - Margot (Sadler's Wells (USA))

046 **MOOHAAJIM** (IRE) 3 b c Cape Cross (IRE) - Thiella (USA) (Kingmambo (USA))
047 **REMINISCE** (IRE) 3 b c Oasis Dream - Sedna (IRE) (Priolo (USA))
048 **RENEW** (IRE) 3 b c Dansili - Hold Me Love Me (IRE) (Sadler's Wells (USA))
049 **REVISE** (IRE) 3 b c Dansili - Niner's Home (USA) (Forty Niner (USA))
050 **SALFORD EXCEL** 3 b f Exceed And Excel (AUS) - Steeple (Selkirk (USA))
051 **SECRET SESSION** (USA) 3 b g Mizzen Mast (USA) - Lynnwood Chase (USA) (Horse Chestnut (SAF))
052 **SEDENOO** 3 b g Cape Cross (IRE) - Eternity Ring (Alzao (USA))
053 **SEMAI** (IRE) 3 gr c Exceed And Excel (AUS) - Mango Lady (Dalakhani (IRE))
054 **SENAFE** 3 b f Byron - Kiruna (Northern Park (USA))
055 **SHALWA** 3 ch f Galileo (IRE) - Kite Mark (Mark of Esteem (IRE))
056 **SPEED BOOGIE** 3 b c Oasis Dream - Wickwing (In The Wings)
057 **SPICY** (IRE) 3 ch f Footstepsinthesand - Shivaree (Rahy (USA))
058 **STRING THEORY** (IRE) 3 b c Medicean - Shebelia (GER) (Black Sam Bellamy (IRE))
059 **SUMMER DREAM** (IRE) 3 b f Oasis Dream - Star On Stage (Sadler's Wells (USA))
060 **SURENESS** (IRE) 3 ch f Hurricane Run (IRE) - Silk Dress (IRE) (Gulch (USA))
061 **TESTAMATTA** 3 b f Motivator - Rummage (Zamindar (USA))
062 **TOP SET** (IRE) 3 ch c Tamayuz - Pray (IRE) (Priolo (USA))
063 **WAKEUP LITTLE SUZY** (IRE) 3 ch f Peintre Celebre (USA) - Maramba (USA) (Hussonet (USA))
064 **WHIPPY CREAM** (IRE) 3 b f Dansili - Diavla (USA) (Bahri (USA))

2 YEAR OLDS

065 **ADERFI** (IRE) 2 b c Pivotal - Princess Danah (IRE) (Danehill (USA))
066 **AL ZAMAN THAMAN** (FR) 2 b c Nayef (USA) - Angie Eria (FR) (Galileo (IRE))
067 **ALEXANOR** (IRE) 2 b c Pivotal - Butterfly Cove (USA) (Storm Cat (USA))
068 **BURSTINGROCK** (IRE) 2 ch g Rock of Gibraltar (IRE) - Second Burst (IRE) (Sadler's Wells (USA))
069 **BYRON GALA** 2 b c Byron - Tenuta di Gala (IRE) (Nashwan (USA))
070 **CHAMPS D'OR** 2 b f Champs Elysees - Shemriyna (IRE) (King of Kings (IRE))
071 **COCKNEY BELLE** 2 br f Cockney Rebel (IRE) - Fustaan (IRE) (Royal Applause)
072 **CRAZY CHIC** (IRE) 2 gr c Exceed And Excel (AUS) - Martines (FR) (Linamix (FR))
073 **DAMASCENE** 2 b c Oasis Dream - Acts of Grace (USA) (Bahri (USA))
074 **DRAGOON GUARD** (IRE) 2 b c Jeremy (USA) - Elouges (IRE) (Dalakhani (IRE))
075 **ESTEBAN** 2 b c Cape Cross (IRE) - Young and Daring (USA) (Woodman (USA))
076 **FINALITY** 2 b c Henrythenavigator (USA) - Dear Daughter (Polish Precedent (USA))
077 **GOLEADOR** (USA) 2 b c English Channel (USA) - Stormin' Home (USA) (Storm Cat (USA))
078 **HAGREE** (IRE) 2 b c Haatef (USA) - Zuniga's Date (USA) (Diesis)
079 **HALATION** (IRE) 2 b c Azamour (IRE) - Ghenwah (FR) (Selkirk (USA))
080 **HOLYSTONES** (IRE) 2 b c Holy Roman Emperor (IRE) - Cappagh Strand (USA) (Grand Slam (USA))
081 **L'IMPORTANTE** 2 b c New Approach (IRE) - L'Indiscreta (Desert Prince (IRE))
082 **LATIN CHARM** (IRE) 2 b c Cape Cross (IRE) - Di Moi Oui (Warning)
083 **LIGHTNING SHOWER** (USA) 2 b c Mr Greeley (USA) - Lightning Show (USA) (Storm Cat (USA))
084 **MAGNUS ROMEO** 2 b c Manduro (GER) - Chili Dip (Alhaarth (IRE))
085 **MANNARO** (IRE) 2 b g Manduro (GER) - Donoma (IRE) (Beat Hollow)
086 **MEANING OF LIFE** (IRE) 2 b c Exceed And Excel (AUS) - Emirates Hills (Dubawi (IRE))
087 **MOONEERA** 2 b f Cape Cross (IRE) - Anna Pallida (Sadler's Wells (USA))
088 **NAADIRR** (IRE) 2 b c Oasis Dream - Beach Bunny (IRE) (High Chaparral (IRE))
089 **NABATEO** 2 ch c Sea The Stars (IRE) - Rosa Del Dubai (IRE) (Dubai Destination (USA))
090 **NOVA PRINCESSE** (GER) 2 b f Desert Prince (IRE) - Nova Scotia (GER) (Sholokhov (IRE))
091 **PELERIN** (IRE) 2 ch f Shamardal (USA) - Fragrancy (IRE) (Singspiel (IRE))
092 **PORTICO** 2 ch f Pivotal - Pediment (Desert Prince (IRE))
093 **QUEEN SARRA** 2 b f Shamardal (USA) - Grace O'Malley (IRE) (Refuse To Bend (IRE))
094 **RASHEEDA** 2 ro f Mastercraftsman (IRE) - Violette (Observatory (USA))
095 **RAYOUMTI** (IRE) 2 b f Lawman (FR) - Sveva (IRE) (Danehill Dancer (IRE))
096 **RED INFERNO** (IRE) 2 b c Tiger Hill (IRE) - Red Yellow Blue (USA) (Sky Classic (CAN))
097 **ROSE KAZAN** (IRE) 2 ch f Teofilo (IRE) - Zahour Al Yasmeen (Cadeaux Genereux)
098 **SALAMARGO** (IRE) 2 b c Sea The Stars (IRE) - Navajo Moon (IRE) (Danehill (USA))
099 **SALFORD SECRET** (IRE) 2 b c Sakhee's Secret - Dhuyoof (IRE) (Sinndar (IRE))
100 **SAYED YOUMZAIN** 2 b c Dalakhani (IRE) - Silver Touch (IRE) (Dansili)
101 **SMAGETA** 2 b f Shirocco (GER) - Sensibility (Halling (USA))

102 **SOTISE** (IRE) 2 br f Shamardal (USA) - Tropical Glamour (IRE) (Rock of Gibraltar (IRE))
103 **SPECIAL MISS** 2 b f Authorized (IRE) - Whatamiss (USA) (Miswaki (USA))
104 **SPIRIT OR SOUL** (FR) 2 b c Soldier of Fortune (IRE) - Far Across (Common Grounds)
105 **SUFRANEL** (IRE) 2 b c Galileo (IRE) - Noelani (IRE) (Indian Ridge)
106 **THE OSTLER** (IRE) 2 ch c Mastercraftsman (IRE) - Awani (Sakhee (USA))
107 **TRIBULINA** 2 b f Dansili - Wickwing (In The Wings)
108 **WHERE DO WE GO NOW** 2 b c Teofilo (IRE) - Persian Sea (UAE) (Dubai Destination (USA))
109 **YEAR OF GLORY** (IRE) 2 b c Kheleyf (USA) - Baila Salsa (IRE) (Barathea (IRE))
110 unnamed 2 b c Invincible Spirit (IRE) - Arbella (Primo Dominie)
111 unnamed 2 b c Green Desert (USA) - Aunt Ruby (USA) (Rubiano (USA))
112 unnamed 2 b f Myboycharlie (IRE) - Eurolink Artemis (Common Grounds)
113 unnamed 2 b c Exceed And Excel (AUS) - Gwyneth (Zafonic (USA))
114 unnamed 2 b c Amadeus Wolf - Helen Wells (IRE) (Sadler's Wells (USA))
115 unnamed 2 ch f More Than Ready (USA) - Jade Aspen (USA) (Jade Hunter (USA))
116 unnamed 2 ch f Tagula (IRE) - Joyful Tears (IRE) (Barathea (IRE))
117 unnamed 2 b c Footstepsinthesand - Kocooning (IRE) (King's Best (USA))
118 unnamed 2 ch c Art Connoisseur (IRE) - Musical Review (UAE) (Jade Robbery (USA))
119 unnamed 2 gr c Teofilo (IRE) - Netrebko (IRE) (Linamix (FR))
120 unnamed 2 b c Galileo (IRE) - Night Woman (GER) (Monsun (GER))
121 unnamed 2 b c Exceed And Excel (AUS) - Norfolk Broads (IRE) (Noverre (USA))
122 unnamed 2 ch f Captain Gerrard (IRE) - Obsessive Secret (IRE) (Grand Lodge (USA))
123 unnamed 2 b c Captain Gerrard (IRE) - Plum Blossom (Beat All (USA))
124 unnamed 2 b c Teofilo (IRE) - Poppets Sweetlove (Foxhound (USA))
125 unnamed 2 b f Amadeus Wolf - Ryninch (IRE) (Dr Devious (IRE))
126 unnamed 2 b c Amadeus Wolf - Secret Justice (USA) (Lit de Justice (USA))
127 unnamed 2 br c Sea The Stars (IRE) - Silent Heir (AUS) (Sunday Silence (USA))
128 unnamed 2 gr ro c Mastercraftsman (IRE) - Sparkle of Stones (FR) (Sadler's Wells (USA))

Clive Brittain

Carlburg Stables, 49 Bury Road, Newmarket CB8 7BY

Tel: (Home) 01638 663739 **Fax:** 01638 661744 **Mobile:** 07785 302121

OLDER HORSES

001 **AFKAR** (IRE) 5 b g Invincible Spirit (IRE) - Indienne (IRE) (Indian Ridge)
002 **AMTHAL** (IRE) 4 b f Dalakhani (IRE) - Al Ihtithar (IRE) (Barathea (IRE))
003 **CAPE ALEX** 4 b f Cape Cross (IRE) - Alexander Three D (IRE) (Pennekamp (USA))
004 **DAGHASH** 4 b c Tiger Hill (IRE) - Zibet (Kris)
005 **HADAJ** 4 b g Green Desert (USA) - My Amalie (IRE) (Galileo (IRE))
006 **MANOMINE** 4 b g Manduro (GER) - Fascinating Hill (FR) (Danehill (USA))
007 **MIBLISH** 4 b c Teofilo (IRE) - Triton Dance (IRE) (Hector Protector (USA))
008 **MUDHISH** (IRE) 8 b g Lujain (USA) - Silver Satire (Dr Fong (USA))
009 **MUZHIL** (IRE) 4 b f Manduro (GER) - Mazuna (IRE) (Cape Cross (IRE))
010 **QUIXOTE** 4 ch g Singspiel (IRE) - Rainbow Queen (FR) (Spectrum (IRE))
011 **RED AGGRESSOR** (IRE) 4 b g Red Clubs (IRE) - Snap Crackle Pop (IRE) (Statoblest)
012 **RUBBAMAA** 4 b f Singspiel (IRE) - Lady Hen (Efisio)
013 **SEMAYYEL** (IRE) 4 b f Green Desert (USA) - Lii Najma (Medicean)

3 YEAR OLDS

014 **ARJAWAN** 3 b g Byron - Al Hawa (USA) (Gulch (USA))
015 **ASEELA** (IRE) 3 b f Teofilo (IRE) - Valse Mystique (IRE) (Grand Lodge (USA))
016 **BOOKTHEBAND** (IRE) 3 ch c Dubawi (IRE) - Songbook (Singspiel (IRE))
017 **HADEEYA** 3 b f Oratorio (IRE) - Pivotting (Pivotal)
018 **HASANAN** 3 b f Rail Link - Dance Solo (Sadler's Wells (USA))
019 **JATHABAH** (IRE) 3 b f Singspiel (IRE) - Zibet (Kris)
020 **MASARAH** (IRE) 3 b f Cape Cross (IRE) - Fragrancy (IRE) (Singspiel (IRE))
021 **RITAACH** (IRE) 3 b f Compton Place - Golubitsa (IRE) (Bluebird (USA))
022 **SADFIG** 3 b c Notnowcato - Coconut Queen (IRE) (Alhaarth (IRE))
023 **SADIIGAH** 3 b f Medicean - Regal Riband (Fantastic Light (USA))
024 **SHAFAANI** 3 b f Green Desert (USA) - Amalie (IRE) (Fasliyev (USA))
025 **SINAADI** (IRE) 3 b f Kyllachy - Quantum (IRE) (Alhaarth (IRE))
026 **TAHAF** (IRE) 3 b c Authorized (IRE) - Lady Zonda (Lion Cavern (USA))
027 **TUFFAN** (USA) 3 b g Bernardini (USA) - Love of Dubai (USA) (More Than Ready (USA))
028 unnamed 3 b f Manduro (GER) - Bunting (Shaadi (USA))
029 unnamed 3 b br c Kheleyf (USA) - Snap Crackle Pop (IRE) (Statoblest)

2 YEAR OLDS

030 **ACCLIO** (IRE) 2 b f Acclamation - Hovering (IRE) (In The Wings)
031 **AQLAAM VISION** 2 b f Aqlaam - Dream Vision (USA) (Distant View (USA))
032 **AQUALUNA** 2 b c Aqlaam - Sirena (GER) (Tejano (USA))
033 **BAHAMIAN HEIGHTS** 2 b c Bahamian Bounty - Tahirah (Green Desert (USA))
034 **BUSH BEAUTY** (IRE) 2 b f Bushranger (IRE) - Scottendale (Zilzal (USA))
035 **BUSH BRANCH** (IRE) 2 b f Bushranger (IRE) - Trim (IRE) (Ela-Mana-Mou)
036 **CADEAUX POWER** 2 b f Major Cadeaux - Right Answer (Lujain (USA))
037 **CAPE CASTLE** (IRE) 2 b f Cape Cross (IRE) - Kaabari (USA) (Seeking The Gold (USA))
038 **CAPELENA** 2 b f Cape Cross (IRE) - Roslea Lady (IRE) (Alhaarth (IRE))
039 **CAPELITA** 2 b f Cape Cross (IRE) - Zamhrear (Singspiel (IRE))
040 **DALAKI** (IRE) 2 b c Dalakhani (IRE) - Lunda (IRE) (Soviet Star (USA))
041 **DANCE BID** 2 b f Authorized (IRE) - Dancing Fire (USA) (Dayjur (USA))
042 **DANCEALOT** 2 b f Lawman (FR) - Dance of Light (USA) (Sadler's Wells (USA))
043 **DREAM AND HOPE** 2 b f Royal Applause - Senta's Dream (Danehill (USA))
044 **IFRIKA** 2 ch f Iffraaj - Poyle Caitlin (IRE) (Bachir (IRE))
045 **INTIMIDATOR** (IRE) 2 b c Intikhab (USA) - Zither (Zafonic (USA))

GROVE FARM STUD

GROVE FARM STUD, WICKHAMBROOK, NEWMARKET, SUFFOLK, CB8 8YA
Telephone: 01440 820395 Fax: 01440 821946
Web Site: www.grovefarmstud.com
e-mail address: julian@grovefarmstud.com

Stud Owner: Julian Wilson (Mobile: 07747-761596)

Stud Manager: Anne Wilson (Mobile: 07747-761597)

100 acres

Accommodation for 50 horses

Brief History: Established in 1986.

Facilities include: CCtv, vet handling stocks, a 45ft horsewalker, our own horsebox.

GROVE FARM STUD takes mares, foals, yearlings and horses out of training.

Resting racehorses (including colts) are welcomed (Individual turn out).

Isolation yard available, for foreign travel.

Stud Record:
Grove Farm Stud has bred/raised the winners of over 300 races worldwide, including 2012 Gr.2 German 1000 Guineas winner **ELECTRELANE**, the dual Gr.1 winner **EUROPA POINT**, Group winner **IVER BRIDGE LAD**, Group-placed **Night Lily**, Listed winners **Terra di Tuffi** in Germany; **Riviersonderend** in South Africa and stakes performers **Imperialistic Diva** and **Golden Anthem** in the UK.

Five Racing Post Yearling Bonus winners 2010-12.

046 **MEDALLERO** (USA) 2 b c Medaglia d'Oro (USA) - Rajeem (Diktat)
047 **NEW CAT** (IRE) 2 b c New Approach (IRE) - Bush Cat (USA) (Kingmambo (USA))
048 **PASTORAL WITNESS** 2 b f Pastoral Pursuits - Witness (Efisio)
049 **RIZEENA** (IRE) 2 b f Iffraaj - Serena's Storm (IRE) (Statue of Liberty (USA))
050 **SLEEPING PRINCESS** (IRE) 2 ch f Dalakhani (IRE) - Savignano (Polish Precedent (USA))
051 **STREET FORCE** (USA) 2 b c Street Cry (IRE) - Maskunah (IRE) (Sadler's Wells (USA))
052 **SURETY** (IRE) 2 b c Cape Cross (IRE) - Guarantia (Selkirk (USA))
053 **WEEKEND GETAWAY** (IRE) 2 b f Acclamation - Week End (Selkirk (USA))
054 **YUKON GIRL** (IRE) 2 b f Manduro (GER) - Yukon Hope (USA) (Forty Niner (USA))
055 unnamed 2 ch f New Approach (IRE) - Calakanga (Dalakhani (IRE))
056 unnamed 2 b c Teofilo (IRE) - Clear Voice (USA) (Cryptoclearance (USA))
057 unnamed 2 b f Cape Cross (IRE) - Fann (USA) (Diesis)
058 unnamed 2 ch c Piccolo - Fleeting Moon (Fleetwood (IRE))
059 unnamed 2 b c Cape Cross (IRE) - Lady Zonda (Lion Cavern (USA))
060 unnamed 2 b f Medaglia d'Oro (USA) - Love of Dubai (USA) (More Than Ready (USA))
061 unnamed 2 b c Dandy Man (IRE) - Miss Demure (Shy Groom (USA))
062 unnamed 2 b c Exceed And Excel (AUS) - O Fourlunda (Halling (USA))
063 unnamed 2 ch c Halling (USA) - Pachanga (Inchinor)
064 unnamed 2 b f Kyllachy - Precious Secret (IRE) (Fusaichi Pegasus (USA))
065 unnamed 2 b f Medicean - Qui Moi (CAN) (Swain (IRE))
066 unnamed 2 b f Major Cadeaux - Quiz Show (Primo Dominie)
067 unnamed 2 b c Authorized (IRE) - Red Blooded Woman (USA) (Red Ransom (USA))
068 unnamed 2 ch c Virtual - Rosabee (IRE) (No Excuse Needed)
069 unnamed 2 b c Teofilo (IRE) - Samdaniya (Machiavellian (USA))
070 unnamed 2 b c Dubawi (IRE) - Scotch Bonnet (IRE) (Montjeu (IRE))
071 unnamed 2 gr c Clodovil (IRE) - Shambodia (IRE) (Petardia)
072 unnamed 2 b c New Approach (IRE) - Shimna (Mr Prospector (USA))
073 unnamed 2 b f Royal Applause - Tarbiyah (Singspiel (IRE))
074 unnamed 2 b f Halling (USA) - Tithcar (Cadeaux Genereux)
075 unnamed 2 b f Invincible Spirit (IRE) - Wing Stealth (IRE) (Hawk Wing (USA))

Clutterbucks
RESTAURANT AT THE WHEATSHEAF

The Wheatsheaf

45 Chapel Street · Exning · Newmarket · Suffolk · CB8 7HA

Tel: 01638 577237

The Wheatsheaf Inn at Exning, Newmarket, a Bed and Breakast and Public House, is a five minute drive from the flat racing headquarters and also the famous Tattersalls sales.

Nestling in the centre of the village, the Wheatsheaf (a 17th century Inn) is situated in superb gardens. Under the care and attention of Ken Clutterbuck it is a thriving village pub offering great food and peace and quiet. It is ideal for the racegoer, for short breaks or business stays.

Have a quiet drink with visitors and locals and enjoy the delicious home prepared food, real ales and savour the atmosphere of a racing pub.

The pub balances gentle modernisation with traditional charm, the bar is friendly and lively, yet with space enough for quiet conversation.

Check out our website for details
www.wheatsheafexning.co.uk

Find us on Facebook

Andi Brown

SOUTHFIELDS STABLES, HAMILTON ROAD, NEWMARKET, SUFFOLK, CB8 7JQ

Tel: 01638 **Fax:** 01638 **Mobile:** 07

NO HORSE LIST AVAILABLE AT TIME OF GOING TO PRESS

Gerard Butler

Main Yard, Egerton House Stables, Cambridge Road, Newmarket CB8 0TH

Tel: 01638 666292 **Fax:** 01638 666292 **Mobile:** 07973 715122

NO HORSE LIST AVAILABLE AT TIME OF GOING TO PRESS

John Butler

THE BUNGALOW CHARNWOOD STABLES HAMILTON ROAD NEWMARKET CB8 7JQ
Mobile: 07764 999743

OLDER HORSES

001 **ALBERT TATLOCK** (IRE) 4 b g Antonius Pius (USA) - Double Precedent (Polish Precedent (USA))
002 **MR LOVER LOVER** (IRE) 4 b g Catcher In The Rye (IRE) - Lovingit (IRE) (Fasliyev (USA))
003 **SALOOMY** 4 ch c Shamardal (USA) - Oystermouth (Averti (IRE))

3 YEAR OLDS

004 **ALSAQI** (IRE) 3 b g Singspiel (IRE) - Oriental Dance (Fantastic Light (USA))
005 **BENIM** 3 b f Authorized (IRE) - Princess Danah (IRE) (Danehill (USA))
006 **COMMON COURTESY** 3 b f Motivator - Crystal Swan (IRE) (Dalakhani (IRE))
007 **LILLY WHITE** (USA) 3 b f Speightstown (USA) - Unrestrained (USA) (Unbridled (USA))
008 **RED EIGHT** (USA) 3 b br c Gone West (USA) - Katherine Seymour (Green Desert (USA))
009 **SWORD OF THE LORD** 3 b g Kheleyf (USA) - Blue Echo (Kyllachy)

2 YEAR OLDS

010 unnamed 2 b c Tagula (IRE) - Cape Sydney (IRE) (Cape Cross (IRE))
011 unnamed 2 b c Araafa (IRE) - Contradictive (USA) (Kingmambo (USA))
012 unnamed 2 b c High Chaparral (IRE) - Green Castle (IRE) (Indian Ridge)

Don Cantillon

Hackness Villa Stables, 63 Exeter Road, Newmarket CB8 8LP
Correspondence to Seymour House, 10-12 Rous Road, Newmarket CB8 8DL

Tel: 01638 668507 **Mobile:** 07709 377601 **Fax:** 01638 668507

NO HORSE LIST AVAILABLE AT TIME OF GOING TO PRESS

Anthony Carson

Main Yard, Southgate Stables, Hamilton Road, Newmarket CB8 0WY

Tel: 01638 660947 **Mobile:** 07977 060064

OLDER HORSES

001 **AMIS REUNIS** 4 b f Bahamian Bounty - Spring Clean (FR) (Danehill (USA))
002 **BRIMSTONE HILL** (IRE) 4 b c Royal Applause - Right As Rain (Rainbow Quest (USA))
003 **DASHWOOD** 6 b g Pivotal - Most Charming (FR) (Darshaan)
004 **DIVEA** 4 b f Dylan Thomas (IRE) - Cumin (USA) (Fusaichi Pegasus (USA))
005 **GEEAITCH** 4 ch g Cockney Rebel (IRE) - Grand Rebecca (IRE) (Namid)
006 **HAIL PROMENADER** (IRE) 7 b g Acclamation - Tribal Rite (Be My Native (USA))
007 **PEACE IN OUR TIME** 4 b g Echo of Light - Deira (USA) (Green Desert (USA))
008 **PEACE SEEKER** 5 b g Oasis Dream - Mina (Selkirk (USA))
009 **STATUS SYMBOL** (IRE) 8 ch g Polish Precedent (USA) - Desired (Rainbow Quest (USA))
010 **TETH** 4 br f Dansili - Beta (Selkirk (USA))

3 YEAR OLDS

011 **KASBHOM** 3 b g Refuse To Bend (IRE) - Summerstrand (IRE) (Cape Cross (IRE))
012 **MADE IT** (IRE) 3 b f Oratorio (IRE) - Theebah (Bahamian Bounty)
013 **SUN VALLEY** 3 ch f Three Valleys (USA) - Tanasie (Cadeaux Genereux)

2 YEAR OLDS

014 **FINAL COUNTDOWN** 2 ch c Selkirk (USA) - Culture Queen (King's Best (USA))
015 **PIEMAN'S GIRL** 2 b f Henrythenavigator (USA) - Aromatherapy (Oasis Dream)

The Late Sir Henry Cecil

Warren Place, Moulton Road, Newmarket, Suffolk CB8 8QQ

Tel: (Office) 01638 662192 **Tel:** (Home) 01638 662387 **Fax:** 01638 669005

OLDER HORSES

001 **ACE OF VALHALLA** 4 b c Authorized (IRE) - Trick of Ace (USA) (Clever Trick (USA))
002 **BEAUTY PARLOUR** 4 b f Deep Impact (JPN) - Bastet (IRE) (Giant's Causeway (USA))
003 **CHIGUN** 4 b f Oasis Dream - Stormy Weather (Nashwan (USA))
004 **CONTINUUM** 4 b br c Dansili - Clepsydra (Sadler's Wells (USA))
005 **CRYSTAL MONARCH** (IRE) 4 b g Dalakhani (IRE) - Top Crystal (IRE) (Sadler's Wells (USA))
006 **DR YES** (FR) 4 b c Dansili - Light Shift (USA) (Kingmambo (USA))
007 **FIRST MOHICAN** 5 ch g Tobougg (IRE) - Mohican Girl (Dancing Brave (USA))
008 **FRAGONARD** 4 ch f Teofilo (IRE) - Delicieuse Lady (Trempolino (USA))
009 **NOBLE MISSION** 4 b c Galileo (IRE) - Kind (IRE) (Danehill (USA))
010 **RUNNING DEER** (IRE) 4 b f Hurricane Run (IRE) - Sweet Sioux (Halling (USA))
011 **SONGBIRD** (IRE) 4 ch f Danehill Dancer (IRE) - Mine Excavation (FR) (Galileo (IRE))
012 **SPIRITOFTOMINTOUL** 4 gr g Authorized (IRE) - Diamond Line (FR) (Linamix (FR))
013 **STIPULATE** 4 b g Dansili - Indication (Sadler's Wells (USA))
014 **THOMAS CHIPPENDALE** (IRE) 4 br c Dansili - All My Loving (IRE) (Sadler's Wells (USA))
015 **TICKLED PINK** (IRE) 4 gr f Invincible Spirit (IRE) - Cassandra Go (IRE) (Indian Ridge)
016 **TIGER CLIFF** (IRE) 4 b g Tiger Hill (IRE) - Verbania (IRE) (In The Wings)
017 **TORUK MACTO** (IRE) 4 b c Authorized (IRE) - Mythical Girl (USA) (Gone West (USA))
018 **WILD COCO** (GER) 5 ch m Shirocco (GER) - Wild Side (GER) (Sternkoenig (IRE))
019 **WORLD DOMINATION** (USA) 5 b h Empire Maker (USA) - Reams of Verse (USA) (Nureyev (USA))
020 **ZEYRAN** (IRE) 4 ch f Galileo (IRE) - Chervil (Dansili)

3 YEAR OLDS

021 **AL ARISH** (IRE) 3 b g Iffraaj - Flash And Dazzle (IRE) (Bertolini (USA))
022 **AL GUWAIR** (IRE) 3 b c Shirocco (GER) - Katariya (IRE) (Barathea (IRE))
023 **AL WAAB** (IRE) 3 ch c Danehill Dancer (IRE) - Aunt Julia (In The Wings)
024 **AL WUKIR** (IRE) 3 b c Jeremy (USA) - Collada (IRE) (Desert Prince (IRE))
025 **AMELIORATE** (IRE) 3 b f Galileo (IRE) - Arkadina (IRE) (Danehill (USA))
026 **ANEW** 3 b f Oasis Dream - Kid Gloves (In The Wings)
027 **ARCHIVE** 3 b f Dansili - Modesta (IRE) (Sadler's Wells (USA))
028 **ATARAXIS** (FR) 3 b c Nayef (USA) - Seven Magicians (USA) (Silver Hawk (USA))
029 **ATLANTIC ISLE** (GER) 3 b f Tamayuz - All Time Great (Night Shift (USA))
030 **AUTUN** (USA) 3 b c Empire Maker (USA) - Sense of Joy (Dansili)
031 **BEJEWELED** (IRE) 3 br f Rock of Gibraltar (IRE) - Gems of Araby (Zafonic (USA))
032 **BLIGHTY** (IRE) 3 ch c Beat Hollow - Brisk Breeze (GER) (Monsun (GER))
033 **BUCHANAN** 3 b c Dansili - Because (IRE) (Sadler's Wells (USA))
034 **CONSERVE** (IRE) 3 b f Duke of Marmalade (IRE) - Minor Point (Selkirk (USA))
035 **COSMIC CURIOUS** (GER) 3 gr c Rock of Gibraltar (IRE) - Cosmic Fire (FR) (Dalakhani (IRE))
036 **COURT PASTORAL** 3 b f Mount Nelson - Teggiano (IRE) (Mujtahid (USA))
037 **DEMONIC** 3 b c Dansili - Bionic (Zafonic (USA))
038 **DISCLAIMER** 3 b g Dansili - Novellara (Sadler's Wells (USA))
039 **EMPERICAL** 3 b c Oasis Dream - Kalima (Kahyasi)
040 **FINGER POPPIN** 3 b f Haafhd - Quest For Freedom (Falbrav (IRE))
041 **FLOW** (USA) 3 b br c Medaglia d'Oro (USA) - Enthused (USA) (Seeking The Gold (USA))
042 **GERTRUDE GRAY** (IRE) 3 b f Hurricane Run (IRE) - Canterbury Lace (USA) (Danehill (USA))
043 **GHOST RUNNER** (IRE) 3 b c Tagula (IRE) - Ball Cat (FR) (Cricket Ball (USA))
044 **HAMELIN** (IRE) 3 b c Cape Cross (IRE) - Love Divine (Diesis)
045 **HOT SNAP** 3 ch f Pivotal - Midsummer (Kingmambo (USA))
046 **IBERIS** 3 b f Nayef (USA) - Isis (USA) (Royal Academy (USA))
047 **JUST ONE KISS** 3 b f Cape Cross (IRE) - Kissing (Grand Lodge (USA))

048 **KORANTAM** (IRE) 3 b c Galileo (IRE) - Miss Beatrix (IRE) (Danehill Dancer (IRE))
049 **MAGIC OF REALITY** (FR) 3 ch f Galileo (IRE) - Breathe (FR) (Ocean of Wisdom (USA))
050 **MIGHTY YAR** (IRE) 3 gr c Teofilo (IRE) - Karaliyfa (IRE) (Kahyasi)
051 **MISFER** 3 ch c Byron - Diliza (Dilum (USA))
052 **MISSED CALL** (IRE) 3 b f Authorized (IRE) - Incoming Call (USA) (Red Ransom (USA))
053 **MORPHEUS** 3 b c Oasis Dream - Kind (IRE) (Danehill (USA))
054 **OPTICAL** 3 ch f Observatory (USA) - Blueberry (USA) (Bertrando (USA))
055 **ORIGINATE** 3 b f Oasis Dream - Sandglass (Zafonic (USA))
056 **PARALLAX** (IRE) 3 b c Galileo (IRE) - Moonlight's Box (USA) (Nureyev (USA))
057 **PERFECT SUMMER** (IRE) 3 b f High Chaparral (IRE) - Power of Future (GER) (Definite Article)
058 **PHAENOMENA** (IRE) 3 ch f Galileo (IRE) - Caumshinaun (IRE) (Indian Ridge)
059 **PHOSPHORESCENCE** (IRE) 3 b g Sakhee (USA) - Eccentricity (USA) (Kingmambo (USA))
060 **RAJARATNA** (IRE) 3 b f Galileo (IRE) - Coup de Genie (USA) (Mr Prospector (USA))
061 **RETIREMENT** PLAN 3 b br c Monsun (GER) - Passage of Time (Dansili)
062 **RIDGEWAY STORM** (IRE) 3 b c Hurricane Run (IRE) - Hesperia (Slip Anchor)
063 **RIPOSTE** 3 b f Dansili - Rainbow Lake (Rainbow Quest (USA))
064 **SAGUA LA GRANDE** (IRE) 3 b c Teofilo (IRE) - Water Fountain (Mark of Esteem (IRE))
065 **SEA MEETS SKY** (FR) 3 b f Dansili - Sacred Song (USA) (Diesis)
066 **SQUIRE OSBALDESTON** (IRE) 3 b c Mr Greeley (USA) - Kushnarenkovo (Sadler's Wells (USA))
067 **TOMINTOUL MAGIC** (IRE) 3 b f Holy Roman Emperor (IRE) - Trois Graces (USA) (Alysheba (USA))
068 **VENUE** 3 b c Beat Hollow - Shirley Valentine (Shirley Heights)

2 YEAR OLDS

069 **AIRFIELD** 2 b f Dansili - Emplane (USA) (Irish River (FR))
070 **BRYCE CANYON** (IRE) 2 b f Galileo (IRE) - Bright Sky (IRE) (Wolfhound (USA))
071 **BUTTON DOWN** 2 b f Oasis Dream - Modesta (IRE) (Sadler's Wells (USA))
072 **CHANTREA** (IRE) 2 br f Dansili - Celestial Lagoon (JPN) (Sunday Silence (USA))
073 **CURVED** 2 br f Oasis Dream - Passage of Time (Dansili)
074 **DORSET CREAM** 2 b f Dansili - Blend (Zafonic (USA))
075 **EQUITABLE** 2 b c Dansili - Honest Quality (USA) (Elusive Quality (USA))
076 **FAIR SHARE** 2 b c Rail Link - Quota (Rainbow Quest (USA))
077 **GALACTIC HALO** 2 b f Rail Link - Star Cluster (Observatory (USA))
078 **HOOP OF COLOUR** (USA) 2 b f Distorted Humor (USA) - Surya (USA) (Unbridled (USA))
079 **JOYEUSE** 2 b f Oasis Dream - Kind (IRE) (Danehill (USA))
080 **KISS OF SPRING** (IRE) 2 br f Dansili - In The Light (Inchinor)
081 **LAKE ALFRED** (USA) 2 gr c Mizzen Mast (USA) - Brief Look (Sadler's Wells (USA))
082 **METEOROID** (USA) 2 b br c Dynaformer (USA) - Enthused (USA) (Seeking The Gold (USA))
083 **MORNING WATCH** (IRE) 2 b c Azamour (IRE) - Lady of Kildare (IRE) (Mujadil (USA))
084 **NICTATE** (IRE) 2 br f Teofilo (IRE) - Woodmaven (USA) (Woodman (USA))
085 **NIRVA** (IRE) 2 gr f Verglas (IRE) - Nirvana (Marju (IRE))
086 **PERIL** 2 ch c Pivotal - Portodora (USA) (Kingmambo (USA))
087 **POSSET** 2 b f Oasis Dream - Midsummer (Kingmambo (USA))
088 **PROPHETS THUMB** (IRE) 2 b c Fastnet Rock (AUS) - Holly Blue (Bluebird (USA))
089 **PUSHKAR** 2 b f Danehill Dancer (IRE) - Mail The Desert (IRE) (Desert Prince (IRE))
090 **RIVER GLASS** (IRE) 2 gr c Verglas (IRE) - Spartan Girl (IRE) (Ela-Mana-Mou)
091 **ROBOTIC** 2 b c Oasis Dream - Bionic (Zafonic (USA))
092 **SATELLITE** (IRE) 2 b c Danehill Dancer (IRE) - Perihelion (IRE) (Galileo (IRE))
093 **SAVANNE** (IRE) 2 b f Rock of Gibraltar (IRE) - Sevenna (FR) (Galileo (IRE))
094 **SHASTA DAISY** 2 ch f Champs Elysees - Bouvardia (Oasis Dream)
095 **SHE'S GORGEOUS** (IRE) 2 b f Acclamation - Acquiesced (IRE) (Refuse To Bend (IRE))
096 **STERLING RUN** (IRE) 2 b c Oasis Dream - Sarabande (USA) (Woodman (USA))
097 **SUNRISE STAR** 2 b f Shamardal (USA) - Tudor Court (IRE) (Cape Cross (IRE))
098 **SYNAESTHESIA** (FR) 2 b br f High Chaparral (IRE) - I'm Sensational (Selkirk (USA))
099 **TACTICUS** (USA) 2 b c A P Indy (USA) - Visions of Clarity (IRE) (Sadler's Wells (USA))
100 **TOUCH THE SKY** 2 br c Sea The Stars (IRE) - Love Divine (Diesis)
101 **VENEZIA** (IRE) 2 gr c Galileo (IRE) - St Roch (IRE) (Danehill (USA))
102 unnamed 2 b f High Chaparral (IRE) - Brisk Breeze (GER) (Monsun (GER))
103 unnamed 2 b f Invincible Spirit (IRE) - Entre Nous (IRE) (Sadler's Wells (USA))

104 unnamed 2 b f Galileo (IRE) - Jessica's Dream (IRE) (Desert Style (IRE))
105 unnamed 2 b c Tagula (IRE) - Lady Flyer (IRE) (Eagle Eyed (USA))
106 unnamed 2 ch c Camacho - Najaaba (USA) (Bahhare (USA))
107 unnamed 2 b f Notnowcato - Picacho (IRE) (Sinndar (IRE))
108 unnamed 2 b f Rock of Gibraltar (IRE) - Prima (Primo Dominie)
109 unnamed 2 b c Amadeus Wolf - Prima Volta (Primo Dominie)
110 unnamed 2 b c Dubawi (IRE) - Starchy (Cadeaux Genereux)
111 unnamed 2 b c Diamond Green (FR) - Sweet Kristeen (USA) (Candy Stripes (USA))
112 unnamed 2 b c Tamayuz - Wild Ways (Green Desert (USA))

Jane Chapple-Hyam

Bottom Yard, Abington Place, Bury Road, Newmarket CB8 7BT
Correspondence to Rose Cottage, The Street, Dalham, Newmarket CB8 8TF

Tel: 01638 500451 **Mobile:** 07899 000555 **Fax:** 01638 500933

OLDER HORSES

001 **APACHE** (IRE) 5 b g Galileo (IRE) - Charroux (IRE) (Darshaan)
002 **BIG KAHUNA** 6 br g Trade Fair - Pistoia (Alzao (USA))
003 **CAWETT COVE** (IRE) 5 ch h Hawk Wing (USA) - Memory Motel (DEN) (Always Fair (USA))
004 **COACH MONTANA** (IRE) 4 b g Proud Citizen (USA) - Market Day (Tobougg (IRE))
005 **EXCELLENT JEM** 4 b g Exceed And Excel (AUS) - Polar Jem (Polar Falcon (USA))
006 **FEVER FEW** 4 b f Pastoral Pursuits - Prairie Oyster (Emperor Jones (USA))
007 **FLYING TRADER** (USA) 4 gr ro g Mizzen Mast (USA) - Remediate (USA) (Miswaki (USA))
008 **FROSTY SECRET** 4 b f Echo of Light - Raze (Halling (USA))
009 **JUNGLE BAY** 6 b g Oasis Dream - Dominica (Alhaarth (IRE))
010 **MULL OF KILLOUGH** (IRE) 7 b g Mull of Kintyre (USA) - Sun Shower (IRE) (Indian Ridge)
011 **OTTAVINO** (IRE) 4 b g Piccolo - Indian's Feather (IRE) (Indian Ridge)
012 **SASKIA'S DREAM** 5 b m Oasis Dream - Swynford Pleasure (Reprimand)
013 **SECRET ASSET** (IRE) 8 gr g Clodovil (IRE) - Skerray (Soviet Star (USA))
014 **STORM KING** 4 b c Shamardal (USA) - Tarandot (IRE) (Singspiel (IRE))

3 YEAR OLDS

015 **MASTER WIZARD** 3 b c Motivator - Enchanted (Magic Ring (IRE))
016 **NELSON'S VICTORY** 3 b c Green Horizon - First Class Girl (Charmer)
017 **PLANCHETTE** 3 b f Mount Nelson - Cruinn A Bhord (Inchinor)
018 **SKATING OVER** (USA) 3 ch f Giant's Causeway (USA) - Annie Skates (USA) (Mr Greeley (USA))
019 **TOMMY'S SECRET** 3 gr g Sakhee's Secret - La Gessa (Largesse)

2 YEAR OLDS

020 **INJUN SANDS** 2 b c Halling (USA) - Serriera (FR) (Highest Honor (FR))
021 **ROCKWOOD** 2 b c Rock of Gibraltar (IRE) - Hannah Frank (IRE) (High Chaparral (IRE))

If you want your horses to be
looked after as they
are at home then come to
NORTHMORE
STUD
Boarding mares, foals & yearlings
Also offering Sales Preparation
Sue Elsdon Mob: 07753 619880
Tel: 01638 577332
Fax: 01638 577021
e-mail: info@northmorestud.co.uk
www.northmorestud.co.uk

Peter Chapple-Hyam

St Gatien, All Saints Road, Newmarket CB8 8HJ

Tel: (Office) 01638 560827 **Tel:** (Home) 01638 500451 **Fax:** (Office) 01638 561908
Mobile: 07770 472774

OLDER HORSES

001 **CARAVAN ROLLS ON** 5 b h Hernando (FR) - Grain Only (Machiavellian (USA))
002 **KING'S WARRIOR** (FR) 6 b g King's Best (USA) - Save Me The Waltz (FR) (Halling (USA))
003 **MY PROPELLER** (IRE) 4 b f Holy Roman Emperor (IRE) - Incise (Dr Fong (USA))
004 **NEVER PERFECT** (IRE) 4 b g Galileo (IRE) - Dapprima (GER) (Shareef Dancer (USA))

3 YEAR OLDS

005 **AGENT ALLISON** 3 b f Dutch Art - Loquacity (Diktat)
006 **AL MUKHDAM** 3 b c Exceed And Excel (AUS) - Sakhya (IRE) (Barathea (IRE))
007 **ARBEEL** 3 b f Royal Applause - Waafiah (Anabaa (USA))
008 **BOITE** (IRE) 3 b c Authorized (IRE) - Albiatra (USA) (Dixieland Band (USA))
009 **BUCKSTAY** (IRE) 3 b g Lawman (FR) - Stella Del Mattino (USA) (Golden Gear (USA))
010 **CAPE OF HOPE** (IRE) 3 b c Cape Cross (IRE) - Bright Hope (IRE) (Danehill (USA))
011 **DODINA** (IRE) 3 b f Acclamation - Etica (IRE) (Barathea (IRE))
012 **DUDE ALERT** (IRE) 3 b g Windsor Knot (IRE) - Policy (Nashwan (USA))
013 **HASBAH** (IRE) 3 b f Cape Cross (IRE) - Gimasha (Cadeaux Genereux)
014 **HERMOSA VAQUERA** (IRE) 3 b f High Chaparral (IRE) - Sundown (Polish Precedent (USA))
015 **INDIGO LADY** 3 b f Sir Percy - Seal Indigo (IRE) (Glenstal (USA))
016 **KING BERTIE** (IRE) 3 b g Clodovil (IRE) - Jouel (FR) (Machiavellian (USA))
017 **MAXENTIUS** (IRE) 3 b g Holy Roman Emperor (IRE) - Guantanamera (IRE) (Sadler's Wells (USA))
018 **MOCENIGO** (IRE) 3 ch c Refuse To Bend (IRE) - Doregan (IRE) (Bahhare (USA))
019 **OSCILATE WILDLY** (IRE) 3 b f Mount Nelson - Marisa (GER) (Desert Sun)
020 **SARJINSKY** (IRE) 3 ch g Raven's Pass (USA) - Dinka Raja (USA) (Woodman (USA))
021 **SHADY MCCOY** (USA) 3 b g English Channel (USA) - Raw Gold (USA) (Rahy (USA))
022 **ST ELMO'S FIRE** 3 b c Bahamian Bounty - Firebelly (Nicolotte)
023 **TIMELESS APPEAL** (IRE) 3 br f Kheleyf (USA) - Elegant Times (IRE) (Dansili)

2 YEAR OLDS

024 **AL SENAD** 2 ch c Exceed And Excel (AUS) - Waafiah (Anabaa (USA))
025 **ALPHABETIQUE** 2 b f Zamindar (USA) - Almamia (Hernando (FR))
026 **AROD** (IRE) 2 b c Teofilo (IRE) - My Personal Space (USA) (Rahy (USA))
027 **BOY AT THE BAR** 2 ch c Dutch Art - Lipsia (IRE) (Dubai Destination (USA))
028 **CAPE MYSTERY** 2 b br f Cape Cross (IRE) - Maramba (Rainbow Quest (USA))
029 **DIRECT TIMES** (IRE) 2 b c Acclamation - Elegant Times (IRE) (Dansili)
030 **DOGARESSA** (IRE) 2 ch f Mastercraftsman (IRE) - Doregan (IRE) (Bahhare (USA))
031 **ETERNITYS GATE** 2 b c Dutch Art - Regency Rose (Danehill (USA))
032 **FARQUHAR** (IRE) 2 ch c Archipenko (USA) - Pointed Arch (IRE) (Rock of Gibraltar (IRE))
033 **FEMALE STRATEGY** (IRE) 2 b f Holy Roman Emperor (IRE) - Strategy (Machiavellian (USA))
034 **HAY CHEWED** (IRE) 2 b f Camacho - Titian Saga (IRE) (Titus Livius (FR))
035 **INCHILA** 2 b f Dylan Thomas (IRE) - Inchiri (Sadler's Wells (USA))
036 **KATAWI** 2 b f Dubawi (IRE) - Purring (USA) (Mountain Cat (USA))
037 **KEY TO VICTORY** (USA) 2 ch c English Channel (USA) - Treysta (USA) (Belong To Me (USA))
038 **KICKING THE CAN** (IRE) 2 gr c Aussie Rules (USA) - Silk Meadow (IRE) (Barathea (IRE))
039 **MAJESTIC SUN** (IRE) 2 b c King's Best (USA) - Shining Vale (USA) (Twilight Agenda (USA))
040 **NOBLE METAL** 2 gr c With Approval (CAN) - Grain Only (Machiavellian (USA))
041 **PINK DANCE** 2 ch f Dutch Art - Dance Away (Pivotal)
042 **PLATINUM PEARL** 2 b f Shamardal (USA) - Gimasha (Cadeaux Genereux)
043 **POLAR EYES** 2 b f Dubawi (IRE) - Everlasting Love (Pursuit of Love)

SHARP
NUTRITION
J. Sharp Nutrition Limited
The Grain Store, Station Road, Dullingham,
Newmarket, Suffolk CB8 9UP
Tel/Fax: (01638) 508 008
Mobile: (07802) 236 277
Email:johnsharp@tb-horse.demon.co.uk
John Sharp acts as an independent feed adviser to leading studs and trainers in the U.K. and abroad and offers a full range of thoroughbred feeds

044 **SEMARAL** (IRE) 2 b f High Chaparral (IRE) - Semaphore (Zamindar (USA))
045 **SONG OF ROWLAND** (IRE) 2 b c Holy Roman Emperor (IRE) - Makarova (IRE) (Sadler's Wells (USA))
046 **SPEEDBIRD ONE** 2 ch f Mount Nelson - Good Girl (IRE) (College Chapel)
047 **STEELE RANGER** 2 b c Bushranger (IRE) - Tatora (Selkirk (USA))
048 **STUBBORN LOVE** 2 ch f New Approach (IRE) - Blue Rocket (IRE) (Rock of Gibraltar (IRE))
049 **TANCRED** (IRE) 2 b c Oratorio (IRE) - Mythologie (FR) (Bering)
050 **THIRTY NINE WINKS** 2 ch f Winker Watson - Teia Tephi (Elnadim (USA))
051 **VOICE OF A LEADER** (IRE) 2 b c Danehill Dancer (IRE) - Thewaytosanjose (IRE) (Fasliyev (USA))
052 unnamed 2 b f Invincible Spirit (IRE) - Atlantide (USA) (Southern Halo (USA))
053 unnamed 2 b f Tiger Hill (IRE) - Carte d'Oro (IRE) (Medaglia d'Oro (USA))
054 unnamed 2 ch c Exceed And Excel (AUS) - Ridotto (Salse (USA))
055 unnamed 2 b br f Cockney Rebel (IRE) - Vino Veritas (USA) (Chief's Crown (USA))

Peter Charalambous

6 Barn, Calder Park, Hamilton Road, Newmarket CB8 0NY
Correspondence to 30 Newmarket Road, Cheveley CB8 7EQ

OFFICE/HOME TEL & FAX 663010 **MOBILE** 07921 858421 **EMAIL** camalotracing@btinternet.com

NO HORSE LIST AVAILABLE AT TIME OF GOING TO PRESS

K. F. Clutterbuck

Pond House Stables, Church Lane, Exning, Newmarket, Suffolk, CB8 7HF

Tel: 01638 577237 **Mobile:** 07868 605995

OLDER HORSES

001 **BOBBYOW** 5 b g Bertolini (USA) - Brooklyn's Sky (Septieme Ciel (USA))
002 **COCOZZA** (USA) 5 b g Elusive Quality (USA) - Watership Crystal (IRE) (Sadler's Wells (USA))
003 **NEVEROWNUP** (IRE) 8 b g Quws - Cobble (IRE) (Bigstone (IRE))
004 **ROYAL MARSKELL** 4 b g Multiplex - Socialise (Groom Dancer (USA))
005 **RUM GINNEY** 5 b m Carnival Dancer - Silent Gem (Bijou d'Inde)
006 **UNCLE PELDER** (IRE) 6 b g Pelder (IRE) - Aunt Annie (IRE) (Synefos (USA))

3 YEAR OLDS

007 **SAKHEE'S ALROUND** 3 ch f Sakhee's Secret - Regal Run (USA) (Deputy Minister (CAN))

Toby Coles

THE FAR YARD, PHANTOM HOUSE STABLES, FORDHAM ROAD, NEWMARKET, CB8 7AA
CORRESPONDENCE TO THE COTTAGE, PHANTOM HOUSE STABLES,FORDHAM RD, NEWMARKET CB8 7AA,

TEL: 01638 660769 **MOBILE** 07904 779222 **EMAIL** tbpcoles@aol.com

OLDER HORSES

001 **CAMELOPARDALIS** 4 b f Tobougg (IRE) - Bonne Etoile (Diesis)
002 **DEAR MAURICE** 9 b g Indian Ridge - Shamaiel (IRE) (Lycius (USA))
003 **LYCIDAS** (GER) 4 b/br c Zamindar (USA) - La Felicita (GB) (Shareef Dancer (USA))
004 **PENINSULA** 4 b f Rock of Gibraltar (IRE) - Kayah (Kahyasi)

3 YEAR OLDS

005 **MASTER HAMILTON** 3 ch g Mount Nelson - Oomph (Shareef Dancer (USA))
006 **NELSON'S MUSE** 3 b f Mount Nelson - French Quartet (IRE) (Lycius (USA))
007 **SPEED DATE** 3 b f Sakhee's Secret - See You Later (Emarati (USA))
008 **TIMELESS** 3 b f Tamayuz - Sandtime (IRE) (Green Desert (USA))

2 YEAR OLDS

009 **APTITUDE** 2 ch f With Approval (CAN) - Moi Aussi (USA) (Mt Livermore (USA))
010 **EPSOM HILL** (SWE) 2 b c Homme D'Honneur (FR) - Energiya Sacc (SWE((Exceller (USA))
011 **LA GRASSETTA** (GER) 2 b f Nayef (USA) - La Reine Noir (GER) (Rainbow Quest (USA))
012 **LEALTANZA** 2 b/br f Zamindar (USA) - La Martina (GER (Seattle Dancer (USA))
013 **MOONSPRING** (IRE) 2 gr f Aussie Rules (USA) - Unintentional (Dr Devious (IRE))
014 **NABLUS** (GER) 2 b g Dai Jin - Nouvelle Princesse (GER) (Bluebird (USA))
015 **ORTON PARK** (IRE) 2 b f Moss Vale (IRE) - Notley Park (Wolfhound (USA))
016 **RESIST** 2 b f Rock of Gibraltar (IRE) - Cecily (Oasis Dream)
017 **ROCKED THE BOAT** 2 b c Mizzen Mast (USA) - Jazz Jam (Pivotal)
018 **WINTER PICNIC** 2 b f Oratorio (IRE) - Salpiglossis (Monsun (GER))
019 unnamed 2 b f Champs Elysees - Bolsena (USA) (Red Ransom (USA))
020 unnamed 2 b f Lemon Drop Kid (USA) - Nafisah (IRE) (Lahib (USA))
021 unnamed 2 b f Authorized (IRE) - Priti Fabulous (IRE) (Invincible Spirit (IRE))
022 unnamed 2 b c Pastoral Pursuits - Dragon Star (Rudimentary (USA)
023 unnamed 2 ch c Hernando (FR) - Ryella (USA) (Cozzene (USA))
024 unnamed 2 b c Intikhab (USA) - Winsa (USA) (Riverman (USA)

Robert Cowell

ROBERT COWELL RACING, BOTTISHAM HEATH STUD, SIX MILE BOTTOM, NEWMARKET CB8 0TT

Tel: 01638 570330 **Fax:** 01638 570246 **Mobile:** 07785512463

NO HORSE LIST AVAILABLE AT TIME OF GOING TO PRESS

Luca Cumani

Bedford House Stables, Bury Road, Newmarket, Suffolk CB8 7BX

Tel: 01638 665432 **Fax:** 01638 667160 **Mobile:** 07801 225300

OLDER HORSES

001 **AFSARE** 6 b g Dubawi (IRE) - Jumaireyah (Fairy King (USA))
002 **DANADANA** (IRE) 5 b h Dubawi (IRE) - Zeeba (IRE) (Barathea (IRE))
003 **EMIRATES QUEEN** 4 b f Street Cry (IRE) - Zomaradah (Deploy)
004 **FRANCISCAN** 5 b g Medicean - Frangy (Sadler's Wells (USA))
005 **FURZANAH** 4 b f Dubawi (IRE) - Latent Lover (IRE) (In The Wings)
006 **GABRIAL THE GREAT** (IRE) 4 b g Montjeu (IRE) - Bayourida (USA) (Slew O' Gold (USA))
007 **HIPPY HIPPY SHAKE** 4 b f Danehill Dancer (IRE) - Hyperspectra (Rainbow Quest (USA))
008 **KHIONE** 4 b f Dalakhani (IRE) - Sularina (IRE) (Alhaarth (IRE))
009 **KIRTHILL** (IRE) 5 b g Danehill Dancer (IRE) - Kirtle (Hector Protector (USA))
010 **MANKINI** (IRE) 4 b g Dansili - Fashion Statement (Rainbow Quest (USA))
011 **MOBACO** (FR) 4 b c Slickly (FR) - Lunaa (FR) (Anabaa (USA))
012 **MOLDOWNEY** 4 ch g Dalakhani (IRE) - Danehill's Dream (IRE) (Danehill (USA))
013 **MOUNT ATHOS** (IRE) 6 b g Montjeu (IRE) - Ionian Sea (Slip Anchor)
014 **OUT DO** 4 ch g Exceed And Excel (AUS) - Ludynosa (USA) (Cadeaux Genereux)
015 **ROCKALONG** (IRE) 4 b c Rock of Gibraltar (IRE) - High Spot (Shirley Heights)
016 **SEMEEN** 4 b g Dubawi (IRE) - Zeeba (IRE) (Barathea (IRE))
017 **VALIDUS** 4 b g Zamindar (USA) - Victoire Finale (Peintre Celebre (USA))
018 **ZACYNTHUS** (IRE) 5 ch g Iffraaj - Ziria (IRE) (Danehill Dancer (IRE))

3 YEAR OLDS

019 **ABILENE** 3 ch f Samum (GER) - Altamira (Peintre Celebre (USA))
020 **AJMAN BRIDGE** 3 ch c Dubawi (IRE) - Rice Mother (IRE) (Indian Ridge)
021 **AJMANY** (IRE) 3 b g Kheleyf (USA) - Passarelle (USA) (In The Wings)
022 **BARTACK** (IRE) 3 b g Acclamation - Bentley's Bush (IRE) (Barathea (IRE))
023 **BLACK ROLLER** 3 b c Kavafi (IRE) - Vallota (Polish Precedent (USA))
024 **BONANZA CREEK** (IRE) 3 b f Anabaa (USA) - Bright Moon (USA) (Alysheba (USA))
025 **BOUCLIER** (IRE) 3 ch c Zamindar (USA) - Bastet (IRE) (Giant's Causeway (USA))
026 **CANON LAW** (IRE) 3 b c Holy Roman Emperor (IRE) - Delisha (Salse (USA))
027 **DESERTED** 3 b f Oasis Dream - Tentpole (USA) (Rainbow Quest (USA))
028 **DIAMOND MINE** 3 br gr c Rock of Gibraltar (IRE) - Kassiyra (IRE) (Kendor (FR))
029 **DON PADEJA** 3 b c Dansili - La Leuze (IRE) (Caerleon (USA))
030 **DUKE OF PERTH** 3 b g Danehill Dancer (IRE) - Frangy (Sadler's Wells (USA))
031 **ELECTRA SPECTRA** 3 b f Dansili - Hyperspectra (Rainbow Quest (USA))
032 **ELHAAME** (IRE) 3 b g Acclamation - Gold Hush (USA) (Seeking The Gold (USA))
033 **ENDLESS CREDIT** (IRE) 3 b br c High Chaparral (IRE) - Pay The Bank (High Top)
034 **EVERLASTING LIGHT** 3 b f Authorized (IRE) - Blue Rocket (IRE) (Rock of Gibraltar (IRE))
035 **GREATWOOD** 3 b c Manduro (GER) - Gaze (Galileo (IRE))
036 **HAVANA COOLER** (IRE) 3 ch c Hurricane Run (IRE) - Unquenchable (USA) (Kingmambo (USA))
037 **JAZZ MASTER** 3 b c Singspiel (IRE) - Turn of A Century (Halling (USA))
038 **KIKONGA** 3 b f Danehill Dancer (IRE) - Kibara (Sadler's Wells (USA))
039 **KINDU** 3 b f Pivotal - Kithanga (IRE) (Darshaan)
040 **KITTEN ON THE RUN** (USA) 3 ch c Kitten's Joy (USA) - Personal Odyssey (USA) (Lemon Drop Kid (USA))
041 **LIONHEART** 3 ch c Zamindar (USA) - Victoire Celebre (USA) (Stravinsky (USA))
042 **MAKAFEH** 3 br g Elusive Quality (USA) - Demisemiquaver (Singspiel (IRE))
043 **MALLORY HEIGHTS** (IRE) 3 b c Dalakhani (IRE) - My Dark Rosaleen (Sadler's Wells (USA))
044 **MARKTTAG** 3 b c Manduro (GER) - Makhsusah (IRE) (Darshaan)
045 **MOUNT MACEDON** 3 b c Hernando (FR) - White Palace (Shirley Heights)
046 **NARGYS** (IRE) 3 b f Lawman (FR) - Spesialta (Indian Ridge)
047 **NELSON'S HILL** 3 b c Mount Nelson - Regal Step (Royal Applause)
048 **NORWAY CROSS** 3 b f Cape Cross (IRE) - Queen of Norway (USA) (Woodman (USA))
049 **PARADISE WATCH** 3 b g Royal Applause - Ocean View (USA) (Gone West (USA))

050 **PARKER RIDGE** (FR) 3 ch c Green Tune (USA) - Peinture Bleue (USA) (Alydar (USA))
051 **PETRIFY** 3 b g Rock of Gibraltar (IRE) - Frigid (Indian Ridge)
052 **PLEASURE BENT** 3 b c Dansili - Nitya (FR) (Indian Ridge)
053 **QUANTIFY** (USA) 3 b f Giant's Causeway (USA) - Measure (USA) (Seeking The Gold (USA))
054 **ROYAL BALLET** 3 ch c Pivotal - Dance A Dream (Sadler's Wells (USA))
055 **SAIGON CITY** 3 b g Mount Nelson - Hoh Chi Min (Efisio)
056 **SASKATCHEWAN** 3 ch c Peintre Celebre (USA) - Sarabande (USA) (Woodman (USA))
057 **SHARAREH** 3 b f Sir Percy - You Too (Monsun (GER))
058 **SHARQAWIYAH** 3 b f Dubawi (IRE) - Pompey Girl (Rainbow Quest (USA))
059 **SILK SARI** 3 b f Dalakhani (IRE) - So Silk (Rainbow Quest (USA))
060 **SLEEPING GIANT** (GER) 3 gr c Dalakhani (IRE) - Special Delivery (IRE) (Danehill (USA))
061 **SORYAH** (IRE) 3 b f Shamardal (USA) - Dirtybirdie (Diktat)
062 **SPIETA** (IRE) 3 gr f Shirocco (GER) - Zarawa (IRE) (Kahyasi)
063 **VELOX** 3 b g Zamindar (USA) - Victoire Finale (Peintre Celebre (USA))
064 **VERMONT** (IRE) 3 b c Muhtathir - Venetian Beauty (USA) (Lear Fan (USA))

2 YEAR OLDS

065 **ALISIOS** (GR) 2 b c Ialysos (GR) - Macanuda (IRE) (Slickly (FR))
066 **ALKETIOS** (GR) 2 b c Kavafi (IRE) - Mazea (IRE) (Montjeu (IRE))
067 **BACK TO BUXTED** (IRE) 2 b c Aqlaam - Incoming Call (USA) (Red Ransom (USA))
068 **BRACKEN** 2 ro c Dubawi (IRE) - Belle Reine (King of Kings (IRE))
069 **COMEDY KING** (IRE) 2 b br c Dansili - Comic (IRE) (Be My Chief (USA))
070 **CONNECTICUT** 2 b c New Approach (IRE) - Craigmill (Slip Anchor)
071 **CROSS COUNTRY** (IRE) 2 b c Cape Cross (IRE) - Altruiste (USA) (Diesis)
072 **DIDIEVERTELLYOU** (IRE) 2 b c High Chaparral (IRE) - Reclamation (IRE) (Red Ransom (USA))
073 **DON'T** 2 b f Invincible Spirit (IRE) - Frigid (Indian Ridge)
074 **GALUPPI** 2 b c Galileo (IRE) - La Leuze (IRE) (Caerleon (USA))
075 **IL GRAN CAPO** (IRE) 2 b c Cape Cross (IRE) - Rambler (Selkirk (USA))
076 **JOYS OF SPRING** (IRE) 2 b f Invincible Spirit (IRE) - Sonachan (IRE) (Darshaan)
077 **KINSHASA** 2 b c Pivotal - Kibara (Sadler's Wells (USA))
078 **KLEO** (GR) 2 b f Kavafi (IRE) - Selfish (Bluebird (USA))
079 **LA FAISAN BLANCHE** (USA) 2 gr f Exchange Rate (USA) - Tjinouska (USA) (Cozzene (USA))
080 **LAWYER** (IRE) 2 b c Acclamation - Charaig (Rainbow Quest (USA))
081 **LUNASEA** (IRE) 2 b c Sea The Stars (IRE) - Musical Treat (IRE) (Royal Academy (USA))
082 **MADAME CLOUSEAU** (IRE) 2 b f Galileo (IRE) - Healing Music (FR) (Bering)
083 **MIZZOU** (IRE) 2 b c Galileo (IRE) - Moments of Joy (Darshaan)
084 **MOUNT LOGAN** (IRE) 2 ch c New Approach (IRE) - Vistaria (USA) (Distant View (USA))
085 **PAST FORGETTING** (IRE) 2 b f Pivotal - Brigitta (IRE) (Sadler's Wells (USA))
086 **PATTERNED** 2 b f Dansili - Paisley (Pivotal)
087 **PETTICOAT LANE** 2 b f High Chaparral (IRE) - Barter (Daylami (IRE))
088 **PICK POCKETT** 2 b c Dansili - Quelle Vitesse (Sadler's Wells (USA))
089 **PLEASANT VALLEY** (IRE) 2 b f Shamardal (USA) - Poughkeepsie (IRE) (Sadler's Wells (USA))
090 **POSTPONED** (IRE) 2 b c Dubawi (IRE) - Ever Rigg (Dubai Destination (USA))
091 **RIJM** 2 b c New Approach (IRE) - Astorg (USA) (Lear Fan (USA))
092 **ROSEBURG** (IRE) 2 ch c Tamayuz - Raydaniya (IRE) (In The Wings)
093 **SECOND STEP** (IRE) 2 b c Dalakhani (IRE) - My Dark Rosaleen (Sadler's Wells (USA))
094 **TAP YOUR TOES** (IRE) 2 b c Danehill Dancer (IRE) - Sharplaw Star (Xaar)
095 **TOLMIAS** (GR) 2 br c Ialysos (GR) - Shikasta (IRE) (Kris)
096 **TRIPLE CHIEF** (IRE) 2 b br c High Chaparral (IRE) - Trebles (IRE) (Kenmare (FR))
097 **VIRGIN ISLAND** (GER) 2 b f Peintre Celebre (USA) - Venetian Beauty (USA) (Lear Fan (USA))
098 **VOLUME** 2 b f Mount Nelson - Victoire Finale (Peintre Celebre (USA))
099 **WENGEN** 2 b c Montjeu (IRE) - High Reserve (Dr Fong (USA))
100 **WILLOW VIEW** (USA) 2 b f Lemon Drop Kid (USA) - Time Control (Sadler's Wells (USA))
101 **WISTAR** 2 b c Dubawi (IRE) - Vallota (Polish Precedent (USA))
102 **ZAWIYAH** 2 b f Invincible Spirit (IRE) - Marika (Marju (IRE))
103 **ZOVIOS** (GR) 2 b c Ialysos (GR) - Messini (IRE) (Ballad Rock)
104 unnamed 2 b c New Approach (IRE) - Hyabella (Shirley Heights)
105 unnamed 2 ch f Nayef (USA) - Night Frolic (Night Shift (USA))
106 unnamed 2 ch f Smart Strike (CAN) - Queen of The Night (Sadler's Wells (USA))

Paul D'Arcy

Charnwood Stables, Hamilton Road, Newmarket CB8 7JQ

Tel: 01638 662000 **Fax:** 01638 661100 **Mobile:** 07768 807653

OLDER HORSES

001 **COME ON BLUE CHIP** (IRE) 4 b g Holy Roman Emperor (IRE) - Rapid Action (USA) (Quest For Fame)
002 **DARNATHEAN** 4 b g Librettist (USA) - Meddle (Diktat)
003 **FAST FINIAN** (IRE) 4 gr g Clodovil (IRE) - Delphie Queen (IRE) (Desert Sun)
004 **MCBIRNEY** (USA) 6 b g Danehill Dancer (IRE) - Dear Girl (IRE) (Fairy King (USA))
005 **REDOUTE STAR** (AUS) 7 br g Redoute's Choice (AUS) - Significant Moment (AUS) (Bletchingly (AUS))
006 **SUZI'S A CLASS ACT** 5 gr m Act One - Latour (Sri Pekan (USA))
007 **TEIDE PEAK** (IRE) 4 b g Cape Cross (IRE) - Teide Lady (Nashwan (USA))

3 YEAR OLDS

008 **JD ROCKEFELLER** 3 ch g Sakhee (USA) - Perle d'Or (IRE) (Entrepreneur)
009 **LYRIC ACE** (IRE) 3 b g Thousand Words - Aces Dancing (GER) (Big Shuffle (USA))
010 **MAGICAL ROSE** (IRE) 3 b f Elusive City (USA) - Xarzee (IRE) (Xaar)
011 **PERPETUAL AMBITION** 3 b g Avonbridge - Never Enough (GER) (Monsun (GER))
012 **SMART EIGHTEEN** 3 b g Exceed And Excel (AUS) - Papabile (USA) (Chief's Crown (USA))
013 **TRUE SPIRIT** 3 b g Shamardal (USA) - Petonellajill (Petong)

2 YEAR OLDS

014 **BIKINI CLUB** 2 br f Pastoral Pursuits - Black Sea Pearl (Diktat)
015 **RELATION ALEXANDER** (IRE) 2 ch f Dandy Man (IRE) - Elshamms (Zafonic (USA))
016 unnamed 2 b c Art Connoisseur (IRE) - A L'Aube (IRE) (Selkirk (USA))
017 unnamed 2 b g Champs Elysees - Puzzling (Peintre Celebre (USA))
018 unnamed 2 ch g Virtual - Salanka (IRE) (Persian Heights)

Des Donovan

Cleveland House Stables, Hamilton Road, Newmarket CB8 7JQ
Correspondence: The Beeches, London Road, Newmarket CB8 0TR

MOBILE: 07761 841285

NO HORSE LIST AVAILABLE AT TIME OF GOING TO PRESS

Clive Drew

Fox End, 83 King Street, Rampton, Cambridgeshire CB4 4QD

MOBILE: 01954 250772 **FAX:** 01954 250772

NO HORSE LIST AVAILABLE AT TIME OF GOING TO PRESS

Ed Dunlop

La Grange Stables, Fordham Road, Newmarket, Suffolk CB8 7AA

Tel: 01638 661998 **Fax:** 01638 667394 **Mobile:** 07785 328537

OLDER HORSES

001 **AEGAEUS** 4 b g Monsun (GER) - Ouija Board (Cape Cross (IRE))
002 **BEATRICE AURORE** (IRE) 5 b m Danehill Dancer (IRE) - Mondschein (Rainbow Quest (USA))
003 **BURWAAZ** 4 b c Exceed And Excel (AUS) - Nidhaal (IRE) (Observatory (USA))
004 **FORT BASTION** (IRE) 4 b c Lawman (FR) - French Fern (IRE) (Royal Applause)
005 **GABRIAL'S STAR** 4 b g Hernando (FR) - Grain Only (Machiavellian (USA))
006 **GUNBOAT** (IRE) 5 b g Danehill Dancer (IRE) - Ramruma (USA) (Diesis)
007 **HARLESTONE TIMES** (IRE) 6 b g Olden Times - Harlestone Lady (Shaamit (IRE))
008 **HOMERIC** (IRE) 4 b g Montjeu (IRE) - Al Saqiya (USA) (Woodman (USA))
009 **JEHANNEDARC** (IRE) 5 b m Montjeu (IRE) - Lucky Rainbow (USA) (Rainbow Quest (USA))
010 **JOSHUA TREE** (IRE) 6 b h Montjeu (IRE) - Madeira Mist (IRE) (Grand Lodge (USA))
011 **MAN OF PLENTY** 4 ch g Manduro (GER) - Credit-A-Plenty (Generous (IRE))
012 **MUBARAZA** (IRE) 4 ch c Dalakhani (IRE) - Mokaraba (Unfuwain (USA))
013 **RED CADEAUX** 7 ch g Cadeaux Genereux - Artisia (IRE) (Peintre Celebre (USA))
014 **ROMEO MONTAGUE** 5 b g Montjeu (IRE) - Issa (Pursuit of Love)
015 **SNOW FAIRY** (IRE) 6 b m Intikhab (USA) - Woodland Dream (IRE) (Charnwood Forest (IRE))
016 **SWIFT GIFT** 8 b g Cadeaux Genereux - Got To Go (Shareef Dancer (USA))
017 **TESTOSTERONE** (IRE) 5 br m Dansili - Epopee (IRE) (Sadler's Wells (USA))
018 **THE TIGER** 5 b g Tiger Hill (IRE) - Rafiya (Halling (USA))
019 **TIMES UP** 7 b g Olden Times - Princess Genista (Ile de Bourbon (USA))
020 **UNBRIDLED COMMAND** (USA) 4 gr c Master Command (USA) - Unbridled Betty (USA) (Unbridled's Song (USA))
021 **VOODOO PRINCE** 5 b g Kingmambo (USA) - Ouija Board (Cape Cross (IRE))

3 YEAR OLDS

022 **AFICIONADO** 3 ch g Halling (USA) - Prithee (Barathea (IRE))
023 **AMAZONAS** (IRE) 3 b f Cape Cross (IRE) - Francesca d'Gorgio (USA) (Proud Citizen (USA))
024 **AUCTION** (IRE) 3 b f Mr Greeley (USA) - Exhibit One (USA) (Silver Hawk (USA))
025 **BANTAM** (IRE) 3 b f Teofilo (IRE) - Firecrest (IRE) (Darshaan)
026 **BOLD CITIZEN** (IRE) 3 b c New Approach (IRE) - Claxon (Caerleon (USA))
027 **CONTRIBUTER** (IRE) 3 b c High Chaparral (IRE) - Serisia (FR) (Exit To Nowhere (USA))
028 **EGHNAA** 3 b br f Cape Cross (IRE) - Alzaroof (USA) (Kingmambo (USA))
029 **ELHATHRAH** (IRE) 3 b f Nayef (USA) - Arch Swing (USA) (Arch (USA))
030 **FILIA REGINA** 3 b f Galileo (IRE) - Ouija Board (Cape Cross (IRE))
031 **FLYING TEMPO** 3 b c Royal Applause - Bel Tempo (Petong)
032 **GWORN** 3 b c Aussie Rules (USA) - Crochet (IRE) (Mark of Esteem (IRE))
033 **HANZADA** (USA) 3 b br f Arch (USA) - Chocolate Mauk (USA) (Cozzene (USA))
034 **HIGH TROJA** (IRE) 3 b c High Chaparral (IRE) - Theben (GER) (Monsun (GER))
035 **IHTIKAR** (USA) 3 b g Invasor (ARG) - Ranin (Unfuwain (USA))
036 **INVINCIBLE CARA** (IRE) 3 b f Invincible Spirit (IRE) - Cara Fantasy (IRE) (Sadler's Wells (USA))
037 **JABHAAT** (USA) 3 b f Hard Spun (USA) - Ishraak (USA) (Sahm (USA))
038 **LADY OF YUE** 3 b f Manduro (GER) - Desert Royalty (IRE) (Alhaarth (IRE))
039 **LAMUSAWAMA** 3 b c Acclamation - Intrepid Queen (USA) (Theatrical)
040 **LEXI'S DANCER** 3 ch f Danehill Dancer (IRE) - Ravine (Indian Ridge)
041 **MANDY THE NAG** (USA) 3 b br f Proud Citizen (USA) - Storm to Glory (USA) (Storm Bird (CAN))
042 **MISTRAL WIND** (IRE) 3 b f Hurricane Run (IRE) - Grable (IRE) (Sadler's Wells (USA))
043 **NAAZ** (IRE) 3 ch c Tamayuz - Naazeq (Nashwan (USA))
044 **NABAT SEIF** (USA) 3 b f Street Sense (USA) - Sierra Madre (FR) (Baillamont (USA))
045 **NARDIN** 3 b f Royal Applause - Third Party (Terimon)

046 **OF COURSE DARLING** 3 ch f Dalakhani (IRE) - Whazzis (Desert Prince (IRE))
047 **RED AVENGER** (USA) 3 b br c War Front (USA) - Emotional Rescue (USA) (Smart Strike (CAN))
048 **RED RUNAWAY** 3 ch c Medicean - Gretna (Groom Dancer (USA))
049 **SAXON SOLDIER** 3 br c Kyllachy - Gwyneth (Zafonic (USA))
050 **SEJALAAT** (IRE) 3 br g Kheleyf (USA) - Laqataat (IRE) (Alhaarth (IRE))
051 **SINGERSONGWRITER** 3 ch f Raven's Pass (USA) - Independence (Selkirk (USA))
052 **SPECKLED HILL** 3 b g Oasis Dream - World's Heroine (IRE) (Spinning World (USA))

2 YEAR OLDS

053 **ALQUIMIA** (IRE) 2 gr f Medicean - Cleide da Silva (USA) (Monarchos (USA))
054 **AMAZING MARIA** (IRE) 2 gr f Mastercraftsman (IRE) - Messias da Silva (USA) (Tale of The Cat (USA))
055 **ANIPA** 2 ch f Sea The Stars (IRE) - Anna Amalia (IRE) (In The Wings)
056 **AURORA BOREALIS** (IRE) 2 b f Montjeu (IRE) - Elaflaak (USA) (Gulch (USA))
057 **BIG BONED** (USA) 2 b f Street Sense (USA) - Lizzy Cool (USA) (Saint Ballado (CAN))
058 **CAPE SUMMIT** 2 ch c Tamayuz - Peace Summit (Cape Cross (IRE))
059 **CRADLE OF LIFE** (IRE) 2 ch f Notnowcato - Pursuit of Life (Pursuit of Love)
060 **DOUMAN** (USA) 2 b br g Giant's Causeway (USA) - Totally Devoted (USA) (Seeking The Gold (USA))
061 **FREDDIE KILROY** 2 b c Pastoral Pursuits - Pretty Davis (USA) (Trempolino (USA))
062 **GIFT OF RAIN** (IRE) 2 b f Galileo (IRE) - La Sylvia (IRE) (Oasis Dream)
063 **HANNO** (USA) 2 b c Henrythenavigator (USA) - Archstone (USA) (Arch (USA))
064 **KAAB** (IRE) 2 b c Kheleyf (USA) - Ms Victoria (IRE) (Fasliyev (USA))
065 **KINEMA** (IRE) 2 b c Galileo (IRE) - Bon Nuit (IRE) (Night Shift (USA))
066 **LIFEJACKET** (IRE) 2 ch c Notnowcato - My American Beauty (Wolfhound (USA))
067 **MAGHAANEM** (IRE) 2 b c Acclamation - Shishangaan (IRE) (Mujadil (USA))
068 **MIYACHIKU** 2 ch c Pivotal - First Bloom (USA) (Fusaichi Pegasus (USA))
069 **MUSALAHA** (IRE) 2 b f Nayef (USA) - Gilded (IRE) (Redback)
070 **OASIS FANTASY** (IRE) 2 br c Oasis Dream - Cara Fantasy (IRE) (Sadler's Wells (USA))
071 **PALACE PRINCESS** (FR) 2 ch f Dubawi (IRE) - Queen of Norway (USA) (Woodman (USA))
072 **PERYZAT** (IRE) 2 b f Mastercraftsman (IRE) - Plethora (Sadler's Wells (USA))
073 **RAWOOF** (IRE) 2 b f Nayef (USA) - Tanaghum (Darshaan)
074 **REHANAAT** (USA) 2 b f Daaher (CAN) - Sultana (USA) (Storm Cat (USA))
075 **ROXANNA** 2 b f Myboycharlie (IRE) - Anagram (Efisio)
076 **SHUSHU SUGARTOWN** (IRE) 2 b f Invincible Spirit (IRE) - Landela (Alhaarth (IRE))
077 **TAQNEEN** (IRE) 2 b c Cape Cross (IRE) - Badee'a (IRE) (Marju (IRE))
078 **TASHBEEH** (IRE) 2 b c Iffraaj - Kayak (Singspiel (IRE))
079 **TWENTYFOURSEVEN** 2 br c Sleeping Indian - Anytime Baby (Bairn (USA))
080 **ZAAWIA** (IRE) 2 ch f Elnadim (USA) - Nidhaal (IRE) (Observatory (USA))
081 **ZARWAAN** 2 b c Dutch Art - Develyn (Pivotal)
082 **ZILBER** (GER) 2 b c High Chaparral (IRE) - Zephyrine (IRE) (Highest Honor (FR))
083 unnamed 2 ch f Shirocco (GER) - Call Mariah (USA) (Dixie Union (USA))
084 unnamed 2 b f Dandy Man (IRE) - Fields of Joy (GER) (Waky Nao)
085 unnamed 2 ch gr f Galileo (IRE) - Hotelgenie Dot Com (Selkirk (USA))
086 unnamed 2 b f Medicean - Island Odyssey (Dansili)
087 unnamed 2 b c Dubawi (IRE) - Ivory Gala (FR) (Galileo (IRE))
088 unnamed 2 b c Dalakhani (IRE) - Jamboretta (IRE) (Danehill (USA))
089 unnamed 2 b c Champs Elysees - La Grande Zoa (IRE) (Fantastic Light (USA))
090 unnamed 2 b c Dubawi (IRE) - Late Night (GER) (Groom Dancer (USA))
091 unnamed 2 b c Oratorio (IRE) - Lucy Cavendish (USA) (Elusive Quality (USA))
092 unnamed 2 ch f Galileo (IRE) - Mubkera (IRE) (Nashwan (USA))
093 unnamed 2 b g Sakhee's Secret - Sinduda (Anabaa (USA))

Chris Dwyer

GROOMS COTTAGE, BRICKFIELD STUD, CEMETERY HILL, NEWMARKET, CB8 7JQ

Mobile: 07831 579844

OLDER HORSES

001 **BAJAN SUNSHINE** (IRE) 12 b g Presenting - Tina's Charm (IRE((Hatim (USA))
002 **BIT WINDY** 4 b f Librettist (USA) - Primavera (Anshan)
003 **DUBAI EMERALD** (USA) 4 b/br f Henny Hughes (USA) - Zanoubia (USA) (Our Emblem (USA))
004 **MIA'S BOY** 9 b g Pivotal - Bint Zamayem (IRE) (Rainbow Quest (USA))
005 **PATRIOTIC** (IRE) 5 b g Pivotal - Pescara (IRE) (Common Grounds)
006 **ROUGH ROCK** (IRE) 8 ch g Rock Of Gibraltar (IRE) - Amitie Fatale (IRE) (Night Shift (USA))
007 **SARAH BERRY** 4 b f First Trump - Dolly Coughdrop (IRE) (Titus Livius (FR))
008 **TATTING** 4 ch g Street Cry (IRE) - Needlecraft (IRE) (Mark Of Esteem (IRE)

3 YEAR OLDS

009 **BALATINA** 3 ch f Byron - Primavera (Anshan)
010 **BRYNFORD** 3 b f Sir Percy - Bull's Crown (USA) (Holy Bull (USA)
011 **FATHER FRED** 3 br g Pastoral Pursuits - Gramada (IRE) (Cape Cross (IRE))
012 **GREY POPPETT** 3 gr f Paris House - Maraffi (IRE) (Halling (USA)
013 **HANNAHS TURN** 3 b f Dubai Destination (USA) - Fontaine House (Pyramus (USA))
014 **NOT NOW BLONDIE** 3 ch f Notnowcato - Gretel (Hansel (USA))
015 **WHITFORD** 3 b c Jeremy (USA) - Linette (GER) (In The Wings)

2 YEAR OLDS

016 **BACK ON BAILEYS** 2 b f Kyllachy - Baileys Gleam (Compton Place)
017 **BASIL BERRY** 2 b c Tobougg (IRE) - Dolly Coughdrop (IRE) (Titus Livius (FR))
018 **ROYAL ROMANCING** (IRE) (2 b f Roman Ruler (USA) - Defensive Boast (USA) (El Gran Senor (USA))

Robert Eddery

Robert Eddery Racing, Heywood Place, Hamilton Road, NEWMARKET, Suffolk, CB8 7JQ

Tel: 01638 428001 (home) **Mobile:** 07938 898455

OLDER HORSES

001 **VASILY** 5 b h Sadler's Wells (USA) - Red Bloom (Selkirk (USA))

3 YEAR OLDS

002 **ADMIRALOFTHESEA** (USA) 3 b g Henrythenavigator (USA) - Duchess Royale (IRE) (Danehill (USA))
003 **BEAU SELECT** (IRE) 3 b g Lucky Story (USA) - Practicallyperfect (IRE) (King Charlemagne (USA))
004 **FORCEFUL FLAME** 3 ch g Assertive - Noor El Houdah (IRE) (Fayruz)
005 **FRONT PAGE NEWS** 3 ch f Assertive - Branston Berry (IRE) (Mukaddamah (USA))
006 **QUADRIGA** (IRE) 3 b c Acclamation - Turning Light (GER) (Fantastic Light (USA))

2 YEAR OLDS

007 **CRAFTSMANSHIP** (FR) 2 ch c Mastercraftsman (IRE) - Jennie Jerome (IRE) (Pivotal)
008 **HONEY MEADOW** 2 ch f Avonbridge - All The Nines (IRE) (Elusive City (USA))
009 **ISABELLA LIBERTY** (FR) 2 b f Soldier of Fortune (IRE) - Samsa (FR) (Zafonic (USA))
010 **OLYMNIA** 2 b f Teofilo (IRE) - Diotima (High Estate)
011 **RED OASIS** 2 b c Captain Gerrard (IRE) - Sahara Silk (IRE) (Desert Style (IRE))
012 **RUDI FIVE ONE** (FR) 2 b c American Post - Dansia (GER) (Lavirco (GER))
013 **SHREWD BOB** (IRE) 2 b c Whipper (USA) - Cheyenne Spirit (Indian Ridge)
014 unnamed 2 b f Myboycharlie (IRE) - Alectrona (FR) (Invincible Spirit (IRE))
015 unnamed 2 b c Captain Gerrard (IRE) - Goes A Treat (IRE) (Common Grounds)
016 unnamed 2 b c Bushranger (IRE) - Lady Corduff (IRE) (Titus Livius (FR))

D. R. C. Elsworth

The King's Yard, Egerton House Stables, Cambridge Road, Newmarket, Suffolk, CB8 0TH

Tel: 01638 665511 **Fax:** 01638 665310 **Mobile:** 07771 804828

OLDER HORSES

001 **CHEWOREE** 4 b f Milk It Mick - Jodrell Bank (IRE) (Observatory (USA))
002 **ELUSIVE FLAME** 4 b f Elusive City (USA) - Dimelight (Fantastic Light (USA))
003 **HIGHLAND CASTLE** 5 b g Halling (USA) - Reciprocal (IRE) (Night Shift (USA))
004 **NORSE SONG** 4 b f Norse Dancer (IRE) - Blue Lullaby (IRE) (Fasliyev (USA))
005 **SALFORD PRINCE** (IRE) 5 b g Invincible Spirit (IRE) - Bring Plenty (USA) (Southern Halo (USA))
006 **SOLAR SKY** 5 ch g Galileo (IRE) - La Sky (IRE) (Law Society (USA))

3 YEAR OLDS

007 **BOLD AND FREE** 3 b g Bertolini (USA) - Lady Broughton (IRE) (Grand Lodge (USA))
008 **COCKTAIL QUEEN** (IRE) 3 b f Motivator - Premier Prize (Selkirk (USA))
009 **CORNICHE** (FR) 3 b f Manduro (GER) - Halska (Unfuwain (USA))
010 **DASHING STAR** 3 b c Teofilo (IRE) - Dashiba (Dashing Blade)
011 **EMERGING** 3 b c Mount Nelson - Pan Galactic (USA) (Lear Fan (USA))
012 **FAUSTINATHEYOUNGER** (IRE) 3 b f Antonius Pius (USA) - Tochar Ban (USA) (Assert)
013 **GREAT DEMEANOR** (USA) 3 b g Bernstein (USA) - Hangin Withmy Buds (USA) (Roar (USA))
014 **LAST HOORAY** 3 b f Royal Applause - Dodo (IRE) (Alzao (USA))
015 **LLAREGYB** (IRE) 3 br c Dylan Thomas (IRE) - Tango Tonic (IRE) (Trans Island)
016 **MAID A MILLION** 3 b f Kyllachy - Poldhu (Cape Cross (IRE))
017 **ROCK UP** (IRE) 3 b g Kheleyf (USA) - Kissing Time (Lugana Beach)
018 **SENATOR BONG** 3 ch c Dutch Art - Sunley Gift (Cadeaux Genereux)
019 **SNOQUALMIE CHIEF** 3 b g Montjeu (IRE) - Seattle Ribbon (USA) (Seattle Dancer (USA))
020 **SONG LIGHT** 3 b g Echo of Light - Blue Lullaby (IRE) (Fasliyev (USA))
021 **UPAVON** 3 b g Avonbridge - Blaina (Compton Place)
022 **ZEUS MAGIC** 3 b c Zamindar (USA) - Milly of The Vally (Caerleon (USA))

2 YEAR OLDS

023 **DASHING PRINCE** 2 b c Nayef (USA) - Dashiba (Dashing Blade)
024 **JUSTICE DAY** (IRE) 2 b c Acclamation - Rock Exhibition (Rock of Gibraltar (IRE))
025 **PRAIRIE PRIZE** 2 b c High Chaparral (IRE) - Premier Prize (Selkirk (USA))
026 **SLEEPY SIOUX** 2 b f Sleeping Indian - Bella Chica (IRE) (Bigstone (IRE))
027 **WATER DANCER** (IRE) 2 ch c Ad Valorem (USA) - River Patrol (Rousillon (USA))
028 unnamed 2 b c Jeremy (USA) - Certainly Brave (Indian Ridge)
029 unnamed 2 b f Milk It Mick - Matilda Peace (Namaqualand (USA))
030 unnamed 2 ch f Compton Place - Phoenix Rising (Dr Fong (USA))

James Eustace

Park Lodge Stables, Park Lane, Newmarket, Suffolk CB8 8AX

Tel: 01638 664277 **Fax:** 01638 664156 **Mobile:** 07802 243764

OLDER HORSES

001 **BAAN** (USA) 10 ch g Diesis - Madaen (USA) (Nureyev (USA))
002 **FULNEY** 4 b f Dr Fong (USA) - Postage Stampe (Singspiel (IRE))
003 **GO SET GO** 6 b g Reset (AUS) - Dragon Star (Rudimentary (USA))
004 **HESTON SOUND** 4 ch g Nayef (USA) - Complimentary Pass (Danehill (USA))
005 **SCOTTISH STAR** 5 gr g Kirkwall - Child Star (FR) (Bellypha)
006 **SEABOUGG** 5 ch g Tobougg (IRE) - Sea Jade (IRE) (Mujadil (USA))
007 **SPA'S DANCER** (IRE) 6 b g Danehill Dancer (IRE) - Spa (Sadler's Wells (USA))
008 **TIGHT LIPPED** (IRE) 4 gr g Dark Angel (IRE) - Kayoko (IRE) (Shalford (IRE))
009 **TORRAN SOUND** 6 b g Tobougg (IRE) - Velvet Waters (Unfuwain (USA))

3 YEAR OLDS

010 **GIFT OF MUSIC** (IRE) 3 b f Cadeaux Genereux - Loch Verdi (Green Desert (USA))
011 **HIMALAYAN PEAK** 3 b g Tiger Hill (IRE) - Rosy Outlook (USA) (Trempolino (USA))
012 **LONDON SKOLAR** 3 b g Tobougg (IRE) - Coh Sho No (Old Vic)

2 YEAR OLDS

013 **DANCING ANGEL** 2 ch f Norse Dancer (IRE) - Indian Angel (Indian Ridge)
014 **GREEN MUSIC** 2 b f Oratorio (IRE) - Loch Verdi (Green Desert (USA))
015 **MAJOR CRISPIES** 2 b c Pastoral Pursuits - Nellie Melba (Hurricane Sky (AUS))
016 **NIMBLE KIMBLE** 2 ch f Kirkwall - Lovely Lyca (Night Shift (USA))
017 **POSTAL ORDER** 2 b f Medicean - Postage Stampe (Singspiel (IRE))

James R Fanshawe

Pegasus Stables, Snailwell Road, Newmarket CB8 7DJ

Tel: 01638 664525 **HOME:** 660153 **Fax:** 01638 664523 **Mobile:** 07771 602501

OLDER HORSES

001 **DEACON BLUES** 6 b g Compton Place - Persario (Bishop of Cashel)
002 **EMILIO LARGO** 5 b g Cadeaux Genereux - Gloved Hand (Royal Applause)
003 **HALLELUJAH** 5 b m Avonbridge - My Golly (Mozart (IRE))
004 **HIGH JINX** (IRE) 5 b h High Chaparral (IRE) - Leonara (GER) (Surumu (GER))
005 **IF SO** 4 b f Iffraaj - Persario (Bishop of Cashel)
006 **ISOLA VERDE** 4 b f Oasis Dream - Firenze (Efisio)
007 **LEVI DRAPER** 4 b g Rock of Gibraltar (IRE) - Splice (Sharpo)
008 **MISS DASHWOOD** 4 b f Dylan Thomas (IRE) - Dash To The Front (Diktat)
009 **NOVIRAK** (IRE) 5 gr g Noverre (USA) - Manchaca (FR) (Highest Honor (FR))
010 **PRIMAEVAL** 7 ch g Pivotal - Langoustine (AUS) (Danehill (USA))
011 **SEAL OF APPROVAL** 4 b f Authorized (IRE) - Hannda (IRE) (Dr Devious (IRE))
012 **SOCIETY ROCK** (IRE) 6 b h Rock of Gibraltar (IRE) - High Society (IRE) (Key of Luck (USA))
013 **VILLORESI** (IRE) 4 b g Clodovil (IRE) - Villafranca (IRE) (In The Wings)

3 YEAR OLDS

014 **ARAGOSTA** 3 ch f Pivotal - Langoustine (AUS) (Danehill (USA))
015 **ARDAAL** 3 ch c Singspiel (IRE) - Moonmaiden (Selkirk (USA))
016 **BADR AL BADOOR** (IRE) 3 b f Acclamation - Dani Ridge (IRE) (Indian Ridge)
017 **BOMBARDIER** 3 ch c Manduro (GER) - Lady Stardust (Spinning World (USA))
018 **COSSETED** 3 b f Pivotal - Fondled (Selkirk (USA))
019 **DELICIOUS POISON** 3 ch c Pivotal - Pediment (Desert Prince (IRE))
020 **DON'T STARE** 3 b g Zamindar (USA) - Joshua's Princess (Danehill (USA))
021 **DRAHEM** 3 b f Teofilo (IRE) - Carinae (USA) (Nureyev (USA))
022 **GLANELY** (IRE) 3 b g Exceed And Excel (AUS) - Bon Ton Roulet (Hawk Wing (USA))
023 **GONE DUTCH** 3 ch g Dutch Art - Ice Palace (Polar Falcon (USA))
024 **GREEN MONKEY** 3 b g Green Desert (USA) - Firenze (Efisio)
025 **KNIGHT OWL** 3 b g Rock of Gibraltar (IRE) - Miss Ivanhoe (IRE) (Selkirk (USA))
026 **KOALA BEAR** 3 b f Oasis Dream - Birthday Suit (IRE) (Daylami (IRE))
027 **LOVED ONE** 3 b f Medicean - Embraced (Pursuit of Love)
028 **MAGIC HURRICANE** (IRE) 3 b g Hurricane Run (IRE) - Close Regards (IRE) (Danehill (USA))
029 **NINJA LADY** 3 b f Nayef (USA) - Galaxy Highflyer (Galileo (IRE))
030 **OKAVANGO** 3 ch f Nayef (USA) - Ivory Gala (FR) (Galileo (IRE))
031 **QUALITY ALLIANCE** 3 ch f Dubai Destination (USA) - Allied Cause (Giant's Causeway (USA))
032 **RABDAAN** 3 ch c Sakhee (USA) - Maghya (IRE) (Mujahid (USA))
033 **RED TULIP** 3 br f Kheleyf (USA) - Red Carnation (IRE) (Polar Falcon (USA))
034 **RIBBONS** 3 ch f Manduro (GER) - Sister Act (Marju (IRE))
035 **ROUBLE** 3 b f Royal Applause - Mycenae (Inchinor)
036 **SEA TIGER** 3 b g Tiger Hill (IRE) - Possessive Artiste (Shareef Dancer (USA))
037 **SHWAIMAN** (IRE) 3 br c Authorized (IRE) - Blue Lightning (Machiavellian (USA))
038 **SORN** (IRE) 3 ch g Galileo (IRE) - Dame Again (AUS) (Danehill (USA))
039 **VANVITELLI** 3 b g Shamardal (USA) - Treble Seven (USA) (Fusaichi Pegasus (USA))
040 **WALL STREET BOSS** (USA) 3 b g Street Boss (USA) - Pad The Wallet (USA) (Skip Away (USA))
041 **WEDDING SPEECH** (IRE) 3 b f Acclamation - Wedding Cake (IRE) (Groom Dancer (USA))
042 **ZADOK** 3 b g Nayef (USA) - Panna (Polish Precedent (USA))

2 YEAR OLDS

043 **ANWAR DUBAI** 2 ch f Aqlaam - Ha'penny Beacon (Erhaab (USA))
044 **AQLAAM HUNT** (IRE) 2 ch f Aqlaam - Leopard Hunt (USA) (Diesis)

045 **BARBARY** (IRE) 2 b c Rock of Gibraltar (IRE) - Silver Cache (USA) (Silver Hawk (USA))
046 **BAYNUNAH** (USA) 2 br f Medaglia d'Oro (USA) - Damaniyat Girl (USA) (Elusive Quality (USA))
047 **CAPTAIN GEORGE** (IRE) 2 b g Bushranger (IRE) - High Society Girl (IRE) (Key of Luck (USA))
048 **CELESTIAL KNIGHT** 2 b g Compton Place - Garter Star (Mark of Esteem (IRE))
049 **DUBAI POST** (IRE) 2 br c Dubawi (IRE) - Storming Sioux (Storming Home)
050 **DUBIAN TO** (IRE) 2 ch f Sea The Stars (IRE) - Mrs Lindsay (USA) (Theatrical)
051 **ELIZONA** 2 b f Pastoral Pursuits - Morning After (Emperor Jones (USA))
052 **ENCOUNTERING** (IRE) 2 b g Duke of Marmalade (IRE) - Naval Affair (IRE) (Last Tycoon)
053 **ENSURING** 2 br c New Approach (IRE) - Dynacam (USA) (Dynaformer (USA))
054 **HE'S MY BOY** (IRE) 2 gr c Dark Angel (IRE) - Rose of Battle (Averti (IRE))
055 **HORS DE COMBAT** 2 ch c Mount Nelson - Maid For Winning (USA) (Gone West (USA))
056 **IBO HAIL** (USA) 2 b c Invasor (ARG) - Sayyedati Symphony (USA) (Gone West (USA))
057 **IT'S A YES FROM ME** 2 b c Bahamian Bounty - Valjarv (IRE) (Bluebird (USA))
058 **SAAB ALMANAL** 2 b c Dubawi (IRE) - Caribbean Pearl (USA) (Silver Hawk (USA))
059 **SPIRIT RAISER** (IRE) 2 b f Invincible Spirit (IRE) - Macadamia (IRE) (Classic Cliche (IRE))
060 **SWORDBEARER** 2 ch g Selkirk (USA) - Isis (USA) (Royal Academy (USA))
061 **TAHCHEE** 2 ch c Sleeping Indian - Neyraan (Lujain (USA))
062 **ZMAN AWAL** (IRE) 2 ch f Dubawi (IRE) - Pivotal Lady (Pivotal)
063 unnamed 2 b g Byron - Buena Notte (IRE) (Halling (USA))
064 unnamed 2 b g Peintre Celebre (USA) - Flying Finish (FR) (Priolo (USA))
065 unnamed 2 b c Invasor (ARG) - Lonely Ahead (USA) (Rahy (USA))
066 unnamed 2 b br f Invasor (ARG) - Ras Shaikh (USA) (Sheikh Albadou)
067 unnamed 2 b f Jeremy (USA) - Startarette (USA) (Dixieland Band (USA))

Miss Julia Feilden

Harraton Stud, Lacey's Lane, Exning, Newmarket, Suffolk CB8 7HW

Tel: 01638 577470 **Fax:** 01638 578628

OLDER HORSES

001 **ATTAIN** 4 b g Dansili - Achieve (Rainbow Quest (USA))
002 **AUTOMOTIVE** 5 b g Beat Hollow - Bina Ridge (Indian Ridge)
003 **BETHAN** 4 b f Nayef (USA) - Elizabethan Age (FR) (King's Best (USA))
004 **CHILLI GREEN** 6 b m Desert Sun - Jade Pet (Petong)
005 **ENTRANCE** 5 ch m Iceman - Enrapture (USA) (Lear Fan (USA))
006 **EXOPUNTIA** 7 b m Sure Blade (USA) - Opuntia (Rousillon (USA))
007 **HANDHELD** 6 ch g Observatory (USA) - Kid Gloves (In The Wings)
008 **KHAJAALY** (IRE) 6 b g Kheleyf (USA) - Joyfullness (USA) (Dixieland Band (USA))
009 **NO SUCH NUMBER** 5 b g King's Best (USA) - Return (USA) (Sadler's Wells (USA))
010 **OMEGA OMEGA** 4 b f Halling (USA) - In Luck (In The Wings)
011 **SANCHO PANZA** 6 b g Zafeen (FR) - Malvadilla (IRE) (Doyoun)
012 **SILVER ALLIANCE** 5 gr g Proclamation (IRE) - Aimee Vibert (Zilzal (USA))
013 **SPIRIT OF SHARJAH** (IRE) 8 b g Invincible Spirit (IRE) - Rathbawn Realm (Doulab (USA))
014 **THE DUCKING STOOL** 6 ch m Where Or When (IRE) - Dance Sequel (Selkirk (USA))
015 **VASTLY** (USA) 4 gr ro c Mizzen Mast (USA) - Valentine Band (USA) (Dixieland Band (USA))

3 YEAR OLDS

016 **AL SAHRAA** 3 ch f Piccolo - Desert Daisy (IRE) (Desert Prince (IRE))
017 **AMELIA GEORGE** 3 b f Avonbridge - Tamara (Marju (IRE))
018 **BELIEVE IN ME** 3 b f Bertolini (USA) - Zephrina (Zafonic (USA))
019 **HONEYMOON EXPRESS** (IRE) 3 br f Mujadil (USA) - Royal Jelly (King's Best (USA))
020 **SHEILA'S HEART** 3 ch g Dubai Destination (USA) - Sefemm (Alhaarth (IRE))
021 **TIGER'S HOME** 3 b f Tiger Hill (IRE) - Homeward (IRE) (Kris)

2 YEAR OLDS

022 **BUSHY GLADE** (IRE) 2 b f Bushranger (IRE) - Cladantom (IRE) (High Estate)
023 **PRIMROSE POSY** 2 b f Byron - Manuka Too (IRE) (First Trump)

Mrs Ilka Gansera-Leveque

Frankland Lodge Stables, Hamilton Rd., Nkt CB8 7JQ
Correspondence: 4 The Maples, Snailwell Rd., Newmarket CB8 7DH

Tel: 01638 665504 (h) **Mobile:** 07855 532072

OLDER HORSES

001 **CRYSTAL HIGH** 5 b m High Chaparral (IRE) - Park Crystal (IRE) (Danehill (USA))
002 **JOE SUGDEN** 4 ch g Araafa (IRE) - Mountain Law (USA) (Mountain Cat (USA))

3 YEAR OLDS

003 **BOBOLI GARDENS** 3 b g Medicean - Park Crystal (IRE) (Danehill (USA))
004 **DUKE OF GRAZEON** (IRE) 3 b g Duke of Marmalade (IRE) - Rambler (Selkirk (USA))
005 **TOSCA** (GER) 3 b f Amadeus Wolf - Tamarita (GER) (Acatenango (GER))

2 YEAR OLDS

006 **RAISED ON GRAZEON** 2 ch f Lucky Story (USA) - Graze On And On (Elmaamul (USA))

Patrick L Gilligan

Sackville House Stables, Sackville Street, Newmarket, Suffolk CB8 8DX

Tel: 01638 669151 **Mobile:** 07881 796612

NO HORSE LIST AVAILABLE AT TIME OF GOING TO PRESS

Godolphin

Godolphin Management Company Limited (Saeed Bin Suroor)
Godolphin Office, Snailwell Road, Newmarket CB8 7YE

Tel: 01638 569956 **Fax:** 01638 667661

NO HORSE LIST AVAILABLE AT TIME OF GOING TO PRESS

John Gosden

Clarehaven,Bury Road,Newmarket,Suffolk,CB8 7BY

Tel: 01638 565400 **Fax:** 01638 565401

OLDER HORSES

001 **AIKEN** 5 b h Selkirk (USA) - Las Flores (IRE) (Sadler's Wells)
002 **CAMBORNE** 5 b g Doyen (IRE) - Dumnoni (Titus Livius)
003 **CAUCUS** 6 b g Cape Cross (IRE) - Maid To Perfection (Sadler's Wells)
004 **DICK DOUGHTYWYLIE** 5 b g Oasis Dream - Sugar Mill (FR) (Polar Falcon)
005 **ELUSIVE KATE** (USA) 4 b f Elusive Quality (USA) - Gout de Terrior (USA) (Lemon Drop Kid)
006 **ESHTIBAAK** (IRE) 5 b h Dalakhani (IRE) - Nanabanana (IRE) (Anabaa)
007 **FENCING** (USA) 4 ch g Street Cry (IRE) - Latice (IRE) (Inchinor)
008 **GALLIPOT** 4 b f Galileo (IRE) - Spinning Queen (Spinning World)
009 **GREGORIAN** (IRE) 4 b c Clodovil (IRE) - Three Days In May (Cadeaux Genereux)
010 **HEPWORTH** 4 b f Singspiel (IRE) - Annalina (USA) (Cozzene)
011 **LAHAAG** 4 b g Marju (IRE) - Chater (Alhaarth)
012 **NABUCCO** 4 b c Dansili - Cape Verdi (IRE) (Caerleon)
013 **PROOFREADER** 4 b g Authorized (IRE) - Blixen (USA) (Gone West)
014 **QUESTIONING** 5 b h Elusive Quality (USA) - Am I (USA) (Thunder Gulch)
015 **SKILFUL** 5 ch h Selkirk (USA) - Prowess (IRE) (Peintre Celebre)
016 **STARSCOPE** 4 ch f Selkirk (USA) - Moon Goddess (Rainbow Quest)
017 **SWISS SPIRIT** 4 b c Invincible Spirit (IRE) - Swiss Lake (USA) (Indian Ridge)
018 **TEMPEST FUGIT** (IRE) 4 b f High Chaparral (IRE) - Diary (IRE) (Green Desert)
019 **THE FUGUE** 4 br f Dansili - Twyla Tharp (IRE) (Sadler's Wells)
020 **TRADE COMMISSIONER** (IRE) 5 b g Montjeu (IRE) - Spinning Queen (Spinning World)
021 **WANNABE LOVED** 4 b f Pivotal - Wannabe Posh (IRE) (Grand Lodge)
022 **WILLOW BECK** 4 b f Shamardal (USA) - Woodbeck (Terimon)

3 YEAR-OLDS

023 **ASHDAN** 3 b c Dansili - Bonash (Rainbow Quest)
024 **BLESSINGTON** (IRE) 3 b c Kheleyf (USA) - Madam Ninette (Mark of Esteem)
025 **BRASS RING** 3 b c Rail Link - Moraine (Rainbow Quest)
026 **BREDEN** (IRE) 3 b c Shamardal (USA) - Perfect Touch (USA) (Miswaki)
027 **BRIGHT STRIKE** (USA) 3 b c Smart Strike (CAN) - Seebe (USA) (Danzig)
028 **CLOSE AT HAND** 3 b f Exceed and Excel (AUS) - Classic Remark (IRE) (Dr Fong)
029 **CORNROW** 3 ch c New Approach (IRE) - Needlecraft (IRE) (Mark Of Esteem)
030 **CUSHION** 3 b f Galileo (IRE) - Attraction (Efisio)
031 **DEBORAH** 3 f New Approach (IRE) - Danelissima (IRE) (Danehill)
032 **ETHEL** 3 b f Exceed and Excel (AUS) - Agnus (In The Wings)
033 **EXCESS KNOWLEDGE** 3 br c Monsun (GER) - Quenched (Dansili)
034 **FALSAFA** 3 b f Dansili - Hureya (USA) (Woodman)
035 **FEEL LIKE DANCING** 3 b c Galileo (IRE) - Maid of Killeen (IRE) (Darshaan)
036 **FLEDGED** 3 b c Dansili - Innocent Air (Galileo)
037 **FLYING OFFICER** (USA) 3 b g Dynaformer (USA) - Vignette (USA) (Diesis)
038 **GERTRUDE VERSED** 3 b f Manduro (GER) - Sugar Mill (FR) (Polar Falcon)
039 **GHURAIR** (USA) 3 b c Elusive Quality (USA) - Alta Moda (Sadler's Wells)
040 **HOARDING** (USA) 3 b c Elusive Quality (USA) - What A Treasure (IRE) (Cadeaux Genereux)
041 **LETTERS** (FR) 3 b f Raven's Pass (USA) - Lady Elgar (IRE) (Sadler's Wells)
042 **MAGISTRAL** 3 b c Manduro (GER) - Tamalain (USA) (Royal Academy)
043 **MARTAGON LILY** 3 f Manduro (GER) - Mezzogiorno (Unfuwain)
044 **MONZZA** 3 b f Montjeu (IRE) - Zee Zee Top (Zafonic)
045 **MUTANAWEB** (IRE) 3 b c Tamayuz - Diary (IRE) (Green Desert)
046 **NARMIN** (IRE) 3 b f Pivotal - Ulfah (USA) (Danzig)
047 **NICHOLS CANYON** 3 b c Authorized (IRE) - Zam Zoom (IRE) (Dalakhani)

048 **NICKELS AND DIMES** (IRE) 3 b f Teofilo (IRE) - Neat Shilling (IRE) (Bob Back)
049 **OBSTACLE** 3 ch c Observatory (USA) - Stage Left (Nashwan)
050 **PHIZ** (GER) 3 b f Galileo (IRE) - Peace Time (GER) (Surumu)
051 **POMODORO** 3 ch g Pivotal - Foodbroker Fancy (IRE) (Halling)
052 **POMOLOGY** (USA) 3 br f Arch (USA) - Sharp Apple (USA) (Diesis)
053 **REMOTE** 3 b c Dansili - Zenda (Zamindar)
054 **RUFFLED** 3 b f Harlan's Holiday (USA) - Mirabilis (USA) (Lear Fan)
055 **SEEK AGAIN** (USA) 3 ch c Speightstown (USA) - Light Jig (Danehill)
056 **SHAMAL** 3 b g Exceed and Excel (AUS) - Miss Meltemi (IRE) (Miswaki Tern)
057 **SHE'S LATE** 3 ch c Pivotal - Courting (Pursuit of Love)
058 **SNOW KING** (USA) 3 ch g Elusive Quality (USA) - Cloudspin (USA) (Storm Cat)
059 **SNOWBRIGHT** 3 f Pivotal - Snow Gretel (IRE) (Green Desert)
060 **SPACE SHIP** 3 ch c Galileo (IRE) - Angara (Alzao)
061 **STRESA** 3 b f Pivotal - Bay Tree (IRE) (Daylami)
062 **SULTANINA** 3 f New Approach (IRE) - Soft Centre (Zafonic)
063 **TAAYEL** (IRE) (3 b c Tamayuz - Sakhee's Song (IRE) (Sakhee)
064 **THOMAS HOBSON** 3 b c Halling (USA) - La Spezia (IRE) (Danehill Dancer)
065 **TOAST OF THE TOWN** 3 b f Duke of Marmalade (IRE) - Boast (Most Welcome)
066 **TRAPEZE** 3 ch f Pivotal - Miss Penton (Primo Dominie)
067 **VANITY RULES** 3 b f New Approach (IRE) - Miss Pinkerton (Danehill)
068 **WINSILI** 3 b f Dansili - Winter Sunrise (Pivotal)
069 **WOODLAND ARIA** 3 b f Singspiel (IRE) - Magic Tree (UAE) (Timber Country)

2-YEAR-OLDS

070 **ALLEGRIA** (IRE) 2 gr f Dalakhani (IRE) - Driifting (IRE) (Sadler's Wells)
071 **BAHA** 2 b c Dubawi (IRE) - Anamato (AUS) (Redoute's Choice)
072 **ANGELIC AIR** 2 b f Oasis Dream - Innocent Air (Galileo)
073 **ASTRONOMOS** 2 b c New Approach (IRE) - Crimson Ribbon (USA) (Lemon Drop Kid)
074 **BEN HALL** (IRE) 2 b c Bushranger (IRE) - Sassy Gal (IRE) (King's Best)
075 **BEYOND SMART** 2 br c Smart Strike (CAN) - Beyond the Waves (USA) (Ocean Crest)
076 **BLOSSOM LANE** 2 ch f New Approach (IRE) - Monturani (IRE) (Indian Ridge)
077 **CORDIAL** 2 b f Oasis Dream - Mirabilis (USA) (Lear Fan)
078 **CRAFTY BUSINESS** 2 b c Bushranger (IRE) - Champion Tipster (Pursuit of Love)
079 **CRITERIA** (IRE) 2 b f Galileo (IRE) - Aleagueoftheirown (IRE) (Danehill Dancer)
080 **DANJEU** (IRE) 2 b c Montjeu (IRE) - Wanna (IRE) (Danehill Dancer)
081 **D'AVIGNON** 2 b c Smart Strike (CAN) - No Matter What (USA) (Nureyev)
082 **DIVISIONAL** 2 ch c Mediciean - Peppermint Green (Green Desert)
083 **DOROTHY** B 2 b f Fastnet Rock (AUS) - Slow Sand (USA) (Dixieland Band)
084 **DREAM MELODY** 2 ch f Selkirk (USA) - Dream Again (Medicean)
085 **ENHARMONIC** (USA) 2 b f E Dubai (USA) - Musicanti (USA) (Nijinsky)
086 **ENRAPTURED** (IRE) 2 b f Oasis Dream - Arty Crafty (USA) (Arch)
087 **EPIC VOYAGE** (USA) 2 b c Empire Maker (USA) - Costume (Danehill)
088 **GILBEY'S MATE** 2 b g Medicean - Al Joudha (FR) (Green Desert)
089 **WESTMINSTER** 2 b c Exceed and Excel (AUS) - Pivka (Pivotal)
090 **PROVIDENT SPIRIT** 2 b c Invincible Spirit (IRE) - Port Providence (Red Ransom)
091 **MINNALOUSHE** 2 b f Lawman FR) - Traou Mad (IRE) (Barathea)
092 **FASTNET RED** 2 b c Fastnet Rock (AUS) - Gyroscope (Spinning World)
093 **FEIGNED** 2 b f Oasis Dream - Factice (USA) (Known Fact)
094 **FINE TUNE** (IRE) 2 b c Medicean - Philippa (IRE) (Galileo)
095 **FOREVER NOW** 2 b c Galileo (IRE) - All's Forgotten (Darshaan)
096 **GAY MARRIAGE** (IRE) 2 b f New Approach (IRE) - Doctrine (Barathea)
097 **GM HOPKINS** 2 b c Dubawi (IRE) - Varsity (Lomitas)
098 **GOLD STRUCK** 2 b c Raven's Pass (USA) - Love the Rain (Rainbow Quest)
099 **GRANDEST** 2 b c Dansili - Angara (Alzao)
100 **HAAYIL** 2 b c Halling (USA) - Early Morning Rain (IRE) (Rock of Gibraltar)
101 **HUNTERS CREEK** (IRE) 2 b c Cape Cross (IRE) - Cinnamon Rose (USA) (Trempolino)
102 **IRISH TEARS** 2 b c Compton Place - Deora De (Night Shift)
103 **JEFFERSON CITY** 2 b c Montjeu (IRE) - Reina Blanca (Darshaan)
104 **KINGMAN** 2 b c Invincible Spirit (IRE) - Zenda (Zaminder)

105 **LIKELIHOOD** (USA) 2 gr f Mizzen Mast (USA) - Light Jig (Danehill)
106 **LONG CROSS** 2 b c Cape Cross (IRE) - Majestic Roi (USA) (Street Cry)
107 **MAHSOOB** 2 b c Dansili - Mooakada (IRE) (Montjeu)
108 **MAKHFAR** 2 b c Bushranger (IRE) - Let Me Shine (USA) (Dixie Union)
109 **MARZOCCO** (USA) 2 br c Kitten's Joy (USA) - Dynamia (USA) (Dynaformer)
110 **MATALLEB** (USA) 2 b c Elusive Quality (USA) - Our Rite of Spring (USA) (Stravinsky)
111 **MAVERICK WAVE** (USA) 2 ch c Elusive Quality (USA) - Misty Ocean (USA) (Stormy Atlantic)
112 **MIHANY** (IRE) 2 b c Teofilo (IRE) - Love Excelling (FR) (Polish Precedent)
113 **MR SMITH** 2 gr c Galileo (IRE) – Intrigued (Darshaan)
114 **MUCH PROMISE** 2 b f Invincible Spirit (IRE) - Prowess (IRE) (Peintre Celebre)
115 **MUNJAZ** 2 ch c Sea the Stars (IRE) - Qurrah (IRE) (Zafonic)
116 **MUWAARY** 2 b c Oasis Dream - Wissal (USA) (Woodman)
117 **NIGHT SONG** 2 b f Oasis Dream - All for Laura (Cadeaux Genereux)
118 **OAKBANK** (USA) 2 b c Empire Maker (USA) - Summer Shower (Sadler's Wells)
119 **OH STAR** (USA) 2 b f Tale of the Cat (USA) - Sleepytime (IRE) (Royal Academy)
120 **PENNY SIXPENCE** (FR) 2 b f Kheleyf (USA) - Zerky (USA) (Kingmambo)
121 **PRINCE OF STARS** 2 b c Sea the Stars (IRE) - Queen's Logic (IRE) (Grand Lodge)
122 **PSILOVEYOU** 2 ch f Sea the Stars (IRE) - Soinlovewithyou (USA) (Sadler's Wells)
123 **RECTITUDE** 2 b f Virtual - Evasive Quality (FR) (Highest Honor)
124 **REWAAYA** (IRE) 2 gr f Authorized (IRE) - Sulaalah (IRE) (Darshaan)
125 **ROMSDAL** 2 ch c Halling (USA) - Pure Song (Singspiel)
126 **SAARREM** (USA) 2 b c Dynaformer (USA) - Effectual (USA) (Carson City)
127 **SACRED ACT** 2 b c Oasis Dream - Stage Presence (IRE) (Selkirk)
128 **SEAGULL** 2 b f Sea the Stars (IRE) - Caumshinaun (IRE) (Indian Ridge)
129 **SEJEL** 2 b f Cape Cross (IRE) - Wajaha (IRE) (Haafhd)
130 **SEMBLANCE** 2 b f Pivotal – Illusion (Anabaa)
131 **SIMPLE MAGIC** (IRE) 2 b f Invincible Spirit (IRE) - Cephalonie (USA) (Kris S)
132 **SOLAR MAGIC** 2 ch f Pivotal - Moon Goddess (Rainbow Quest)
133 **SONA** 2 b f Dansili - Neartica (FR) (Sadler's Wells)
134 **STAR CHART** (IRE) 2 b f Dubawi (IRE) - Star Express (Sadler's Wells)
135 **SWIFT CAMPAIGN** (IRE) 2 b f Intikhab (USA) - Indolente (IRE) (Diesis)
136 **SWISS KISS** 2 br f Dansili - Swiss Lake (USA) (Indian Ridge)
137 **SWORN VOW** 2 b c Yeats (IRE) - Aitch (IRE) (Alhaarth)
138 **TAGHROODA** 2 b f Sea the Stars (IRE) - Ezima (IRE) (Sadler's Wells)
139 **TAWTEEN** (USA) 2 b f Street Sense (USA) - Wid (USA) (Elusive Quality)
140 **TERHAAB** (USA) 2 b f Elusive Quality (USA) - Star of Paris (USA) (Dayjur)
141 **THRONE ROOM** 2 b c Oasis Dream - Magnificient Style (USA) (Silver Hawk)
142 **TOO THE STARS** (IRE) 2 ch f Sea the Stars (IRE) - Finsceal Beo (IRE) (Mr Greeley)
143 **TORNESEL** 2 b c Teofilo (IRE) - Bezant (IRE) (Zamindar)
144 **TRUST THE WIND** 2 b f Dansili - Hypnology (USA) (Gone West)
145 **TWIN POINT** 2 br c Invincible Spirit (IRE) - Gemini Joan (Montjeu)
146 **TYPICALLY TROPICAL** 2 b f Beat Hollow - Tropical Heights (FR) (Shirley Heights)
147 **VENTUROUS SPIRIT** (IRE) 2 b f Invincible Spirit (IRE) - Venturi (Danehill Dancer)
148 **VILLAINOUS** (IRE) 2 b c Pivotal - Infamous Angel (Exceed and Excel)
149 **VOTARY** 2 b c Authorized (IRE) - So Admirable (Suave Dancer)
150 **WARBROOK** (IRE) 2 ch c Tamayuz - Squander (Dr Fong)
151 **WATER HOLE** (IRE) 2 b f Oasis Dream - Arosa (IRE) (Sadler's Wells)
152 **WESTERN HYMN** 2 b c High Chaparral (IRE) - Blue Rhapsody (Cape Cross)
153 **WESTWOOD HOE** 2 b c Oasis Dream - Disco Volante (Sadler's Wells)
154 **WING FOOT** (USA) 2 ch c Giant's Causeway (USA) - Vignette (USA) (Diesis)
155 **ZEPHYR** 2 ch c Shirocco (GER) - Pelagia (IRE) (Lycius)
156 **ZERFAAL** 2 b c Dubawi (IRE) – Dhelaal (Green Desert)
157 unnamed 2 b f Galileo (IRE) - Ask for the Moon (FR) (Dr Fong)
158 unnamed 2 b f Dubawi (IRE) – Cheerleader (Singspiel)
159 unnamed 2 b f Invincible Spirit (IRE) - Crossmolina (IRE) (Halling)
160 unnamed 2 b f Teofilo (IRE) - Emerald Peace (IRE) (Green Desert)
161 unnamed 2 b c High Chaparral (IRE) - Lure of the Moon (USA) (Lure)
162 unnamed 2 ch f New Approach (IRE) - Zam Zoom (IRE) (Dalakhani)

Rae Guest

Chestnut Tree Stables, Hamilton Road, Newmarket, Suffolk CB8 0NY

Tel: 01638 661508 **Fax:** 01638 667317 **Mobile:** 07711 301095

OLDER HORSES

001 **ALICE ROSE** (IRE) 4 ch f Manduro (GER) - Bold Assumption (Observatory (USA))
002 **BE MY ROCK** 4 b f Rock of Gibraltar (IRE) - Supa Sal (King's Best (USA))
003 **ED DE GAS** 4 b g Peintre Celebre (USA) - Sambala (IRE) (Danehill Dancer (IRE))
004 **EVER FORTUNE** (USA) 4 ch g El Corredor (USA) - Beyond Price (USA) (King of Kings (IRE))
005 **FIRST CLASS** 5 b g Oasis Dream - Break Point (Reference Point)
006 **FLYNN'S BOY** 5 ch g Tobougg (IRE) - Bukhoor (IRE) (Danehill (USA))
007 **HEADLINE NEWS** (IRE) 4 ch f Peintre Celebre (USA) - Donnelly's Hollow (IRE) (Docksider (USA))
008 **KALILY** 4 b c Dubawi (IRE) - Mail Express (IRE) (Cape Cross (IRE))
009 **KICKINGTHELILLY** 4 ch f Byron - Teller (ARG) (Southern Halo (USA))
010 **MACCHIARA** 4 ch f Medicean - Castaway Queen (IRE) (Selkirk (USA))
011 **MILIIKA** 4 b f Green Desert (USA) - Miss Anabaa (Anabaa (USA))
012 **MINALISA** 4 b f Oasis Dream - Mina (Selkirk (USA))
013 **MIRZA** 6 b g Oasis Dream - Millyant (Primo Dominie)
014 **POISSON** D'OR 4 b f Cape Cross (IRE) - Lille Hammer (Sadler's Wells (USA))
015 **PRINCESS OF ORANGE** 4 ch f Dutch Art - Radiate (Sadler's Wells (USA))
016 **RIVAS RHAPSODY** (IRE) 5 b m Hawk Wing (USA) - Riva Royale (Royal Applause)

3 YEAR OLDS

017 **CALM ATTITUDE** (IRE) 3 ch f Dutch Art - Turban Heights (IRE) (Golan (IRE))
018 **CAMILLA DE ROSSI** 3 b f Oratorio (IRE) - Supa Sal (King's Best (USA))
019 **FLAMINGO BEAT** 3 ch g Beat Hollow - Flamingo Flower (USA) (Diesis)
020 **HOW'S LIFE** 3 b f Layman (USA) - Get The Ring (FR) (Linamix (FR))
021 **LET'S RHUMBA** 3 b f Medicean - Rhumba Rage (USA) (Nureyev (USA))
022 **NINGBO EXPRESS** (IRE) 3 b f Jeremy (USA) - Sunlit Skies (Selkirk (USA))
023 **ROSIE REBEL** 3 ch f Cockney Rebel (IRE) - Meandering Rose (USA) (Irish River (FR))
024 **SECRET OF SUCCESS** 3 ch f Johannesburg (USA) - Live Life (FR) (Linamix (FR))
025 **TUMBLEWEED FINALE** 3 ch f Tumbleweed Ridge - Poyle Kiera (Diktat)

2 YEAR OLDS

026 **ARCHDUCHESS** 2 b f Archipenko (USA) - Eminencia (Sadler's Wells (USA))
027 **CAPE FACTOR** (IRE) 2 b f Oratorio (IRE) - Crossanza (IRE) (Cape Cross (IRE))
028 **CHESS VALLEY** 2 b f Shamardal (USA) - Grecian Air (FR) (King's Best (USA))
029 **FIRST EXPERIENCE** 2 b f Tamayuz - Lolla's Spirit (IRE) (Montjeu (IRE))
030 **GOD'S SPEED** (IRE) 2 b c Oratorio (IRE) - Guilia (Galileo (IRE))
031 KISS FROM A ROSE 2 ch f Compton Place - Dayrose (Daylami (IRE))
032 **MINLEY** 2 b c Acclamation - Fatal Attraction (Oasis Dream)
033 **MISS BUCKSHOT** (IRE) 2 b f Tamayuz - Miss Bellbird (IRE) (Danehill (USA))
034 **SOUND OF LIFE** (IRE) 2 b f Cape Cross (IRE) - Stylist (IRE) (Sadler's Wells (USA))
035 **STRIKE A LIGHT** 2 gr f Dutch Art - Bridal Path (Groom Dancer (USA))
036 **STROLL ON** (IRE) 2 ch f Exceed And Excel (AUS) - Violet (IRE) (Mukaddamah (USA))
037 **TORREON** (IRE) 2 b c High Chaparral (IRE) - Teide Lady (Nashwan (USA))
038 unnamed 2 b f High Chaparral (IRE) - Distant Dreamer (USA) (Rahy (USA))
039 unnamed 2 b f Aqlaam - Fen Guest (Woodborough (USA))
040 unnamed 2 b f Byron - Flyfisher (USA) (Riverman (USA))
041 unnamed 2 b f Teofilo (IRE) - Jellett (IRE) (Green Desert (USA))
042 unnamed 2 ch g Halling (USA) - Magdalene (Act One)
043 unnamed 2 b f Dylan Thomas (IRE) - Maseera (USA) (Seeking The Gold (USA))
044 unnamed 2 b f High Chaparral (IRE) - Twyla (AUS) (Danehill (USA))

William J Haggas

Somerville Lodge, Fordham Road, Newmarket, Suffolk CB8 7AA

Tel: 01638 667013 **Fax** 01638 660534 **Mobile:** 07860 282281

OLDER HORSES

001 **ARSAADI** (IRE) 4 b f Dubawi (IRE) - Arsad (IRE) (Cape Cross (IRE))
002 **ASIAN TRADER** 4 b g Acclamation - Tiger Waltz (Pivotal)
003 **CONDUCT** (IRE) 6 gr g Selkirk (USA) - Coventina (IRE) (Daylami (IRE))
004 **DANCHAI** 4 gr g Authorized (IRE) - Scarlet Empire (IRE) (Red Ransom (USA))
005 **FAST OR FREE** 4 ch g Notnowcato - Ewenny (Warrshan (USA))
006 **FURY** 5 gr g Invincible Spirit (IRE) - Courting (Pursuit of Love)
007 **GRAPHIC** (IRE) 4 ch g Excellent Art - Follow My Lead (Night Shift (USA))
008 **GUARANTEE** 4 b g Authorized (IRE) - Zuleika Dobson (Cadeaux Genereux)
009 **HARRIS TWEED** 6 b g Hernando (FR) - Frog (Akarad (FR))
010 **HEERAAT** (IRE) 4 b c Dark Angel (IRE) - Thawrah (IRE) (Green Desert (USA))
011 **MAMA QUILLA** (USA) 4 ch f Smart Strike (CAN) - Myth To Reality (FR) (Sadler's Wells (USA))
012 **MUKHADRAM** 4 b c Shamardal (USA) - Magic Tree (UAE) (Timber Country (USA))
013 **NINE REALMS** 4 b c Green Desert (USA) - Bourbonella (Rainbow Quest (USA))
014 **POLAR VENTURE** 4 b g Invincible Spirit (IRE) - Sharplaw Venture (Polar Falcon (USA))
015 **RESTIADARGENT** (FR) 4 b f Kendargent (FR) - Restia (FR) (Montjeu (IRE))
016 **REX IMPERATOR** 4 b g Royal Applause - Elidore (Danetime (IRE))
017 **SENTARIL** 4 b f Danehill Dancer (IRE) - Superstar Leo (IRE) (College Chapel)
018 **STENCIVE** 4 b c Dansili - Madeira Mist (IRE) (Grand Lodge (USA))
019 **SUN CENTRAL** (IRE) 4 ch c Galileo (IRE) - Bordighera (USA) (Alysheba (USA))
020 **WELL PAINTED** (IRE) 4 ch g Excellent Art - Aoife (IRE) (Thatching)
021 **WESTWITHTHENIGHT** (IRE) 4 b f Cape Cross (IRE) - Hidden Hope (Daylami (IRE))

3 YEAR OLDS

022 **AKEED DUBAWI** 3 b c Dubawi (IRE) - Anosti (Act One)
023 **ANEEDH** 3 b g Lucky Story (USA) - Seed Al Maha (USA) (Seeking The Gold (USA))
024 **ARAQELLA** (IRE) 3 b f Oasis Dream - Bourbonella (Rainbow Quest (USA))
025 **ASSEMBLY** 3 ch c Kyllachy - Constitute (USA) (Gone West (USA))
026 **BATTALION** (IRE) 3 b c Authorized (IRE) - Zigarra (Halling (USA))
027 **BOTTEEN** (IRE) 3 b g Invincible Spirit (IRE) - Dundel (IRE) (Machiavellian (USA))
028 **CARA GINA** 3 b f Bahamian Bounty - Princess Georgina (Royal Applause)
029 **CHOCOLATE BLOCK** (IRE) 3 br f Singspiel (IRE) - Pingus (Polish Precedent (USA))
030 **CROSS MY HEART** 3 b f Sakhee's Secret - Sacre Coeur (Compton Place)
031 **DANAT AL ATHEER** 3 ch f Shamardal (USA) - Height of Vanity (IRE) (Erhaab (USA))
032 **DARE TO ACHIEVE** 3 b c Galileo (IRE) - Mussoorie (FR) (Linamix (FR))
033 **ENFIJAAR** (IRE) 3 b f Invincible Spirit (IRE) - Harayir (USA) (Gulch (USA))
034 **ENVIOUS STAR** 3 b f Shirocco (GER) - Star Express (Sadler's Wells (USA))
035 **ESTIQAAMA** (USA) 3 b f Nayef (USA) - Ethaara (Green Desert (USA))
036 **FEHAYDI** 3 b c Nayef (USA) - Red Camellia (Polar Falcon (USA))
037 **FERSAH** (USA) 3 b f Dynaformer (USA) - Jaleela (USA) (Kingmambo (USA))
038 **FLOATING ALONG** (IRE) 3 b f Oasis Dream - Politesse (USA) (Barathea (IRE))
039 **GALEB WARRIOR** 3 b g Duke of Marmalade (IRE) - Katrina (IRE) (Ela-Mana-Mou)
040 **GALLENA** 3 b f Invincible Spirit (IRE) - Emily Blake (IRE) (Lend A Hand)
041 **GHASABAH** 3 b f Dansili - Muwakleh (Machiavellian (USA))
042 **HAIRY ROCKET** 3 b f Pivotal - Asaawir (Royal Applause)
043 **HEROINE REQUIRED** (FR) 3 ch f Muhtathir - Tiger Mist (IRE) (Galileo (IRE))
044 **I SAY** (IRE) 3 b f Oratorio (IRE) - Lisieux Orchid (IRE) (Sadler's Wells (USA))
045 **LADY NOUF** 3 b f Teofilo (IRE) - Majestic Sakeena (IRE) (King's Best (USA))
046 **LEITRIM PASS** (USA) 3 ch c Raven's Pass (USA) - Santolina (USA) (Boundary (USA))
047 **MARTIAN** (IRE) 3 b g Duke of Marmalade (IRE) - Starship (IRE) (Galileo (IRE))

048 **MATROOH** (USA) 3 b c Distorted Humor (USA) - Rockcide (USA) (Personal Flag (USA))
049 **MUNDAHESH** (IRE) 3 ch g Tamayuz - Kawn (Cadeaux Genereux)
050 **MUTHMIR** (IRE) 3 b c Invincible Spirit (IRE) - Fairy of The Night (IRE) (Danehill (USA))
051 **NOBLE DEED** 3 ch g Kyllachy - Noble One (Primo Dominie)
052 **ODOOJ** (IRE) 3 b g Pivotal - Shabiba (USA) (Seeking The Gold (USA))
053 **OUR OBSESSION** (IRE) 3 ch f Shamardal (USA) - Hidden Hope (Daylami (IRE))
054 **PALKIN** 3 b f Singspiel (IRE) - Winds of Time (IRE) (Danehill (USA))
055 **PARIS ROSE** 3 b f Cape Cross (IRE) - Samira Gold (FR) (Gold Away (IRE))
056 **QUEENSBERRY RULES** (IRE) 3 b c Teofilo (IRE) - Fantastic Spring (USA) (Fantastic Light (USA))
057 **RESPONSE** 3 ch c New Approach (IRE) - Spotlight (Dr Fong (USA))
058 **ROCK CHOIR** 3 b f Pivotal - Choir Mistress (Chief Singer)
059 **ROSDHU QUEEN** (IRE) 3 b f Invincible Spirit (IRE) - Green Minstrel (FR) (Green Tune (USA))
060 **SACRED SQUARE** (GER) 3 ch c Peintre Celebre (USA) - Square The Circle (Second Empire (IRE))
061 **SKY GARDEN** 3 b f Acclamation - Superstar Leo (IRE) (College Chapel)
062 **SONG AND DANCE MAN** 3 b g Danehill Dancer (IRE) - Song (IRE) (Sadler's Wells (USA))
063 **SULTANAH HEYAM** 3 br f Manduro (GER) - Royal Secrets (IRE) (Highest Honor (FR))
064 **TANAWAR** (IRE) 3 b g Elusive City (USA) - Parakopi (IRE) (Green Desert (USA))
065 **TRIPLE CHOCOLATE** 3 b g Danehill Dancer (IRE) - Enticing (IRE) (Pivotal)
066 **VALTINA** (IRE) 3 b f Teofilo (IRE) - Vassiana (FR) (Anabaa (USA))
067 **VEERAYA** 3 b g Rail Link - Follow Flanders (Pursuit of Love)
068 **YARN** 3 ch f Dutch Art - Spinneret (Pivotal)

2 YEAR OLDS

069 **ALSHADHIA** (IRE) 2 b f Marju (IRE) - Wijdan (USA) (Mr Prospector (USA))
070 **AMNESIA** (IRE) 2 b f Invincible Spirit (IRE) - Applauded (IRE) (Royal Applause)
071 **ARCTIC BRAVE** 2 ch c Teofilo (IRE) - Arctic Char (Polar Falcon (USA))
072 **BELAHODOOD** 2 b c New Approach (IRE) - Broken Peace (USA) (Devil's Bag (USA))
073 **BEST TAMAYUZ** 2 ch c Tamayuz - Pink Ivory (Sakhee (USA))
074 **BILIMBI** (IRE) 2 b c Duke of Marmalade (IRE) - Starship (IRE) (Galileo (IRE))
075 **BUREDYMA** 2 ch f Dutch Art - Petong's Pet (Petong)
076 **DANEHILL REVIVAL** 2 b f Pivotal - Danehill Destiny (Danehill Dancer (IRE))
077 **DREAM SPIRIT** (IRE) 2 b c Invincible Spirit (IRE) - Dream Valley (IRE) (Sadler's Wells (USA))
078 **DUTCH DAWN** 2 b f Dutch Art - Shebaan (Compton Place)
079 **EHTIFAAL** (IRE) 2 b c Teofilo (IRE) - Kashoof (Green Desert (USA))
080 **ELHAAM** (IRE) 2 b f Shamardal (USA) - Loulwa (IRE) (Montjeu (IRE))
081 **ERTIJAAL** (IRE) 2 b c Oasis Dream - Shabiba (USA) (Seeking The Gold (USA))
082 **ETAAB** (USA) 2 b f Street Cry (IRE) - Ethaara (Green Desert (USA))
083 **EXAMINER** (IRE) 2 ch g Excellent Art - Therry Girl (IRE) (Lahib (USA))
084 **FAWN** 2 ch f Selkirk (USA) - Blue Dream (IRE) (Cadeaux Genereux)
085 **FELWAH** 2 ch f Aqlaam - Efisio's Star (Efisio)
086 **FLIPPANT** (IRE) 2 ch f Pivotal - Moon Dazzle (USA) (Kingmambo (USA))
087 **FRENCH FRIEND** (IRE) 2 b f Teofilo (IRE) - Mayenne (USA) (Nureyev (USA))
088 **GOLD APPROACH** 2 ch f New Approach (IRE) - Samira Gold (FR) (Gold Away (IRE))
089 **GRASS GREEN** 2 b f Dubawi (IRE) - Grasshoppergreen (IRE) (Barathea (IRE))
090 **HAIKBIDIAC** (IRE) 2 b c Kodiac - Silk Fan (IRE) (Unfuwain (USA))
091 **KAHEYLL** 2 br c Pastoral Pursuits - Dansa Queen (Dansili)
092 **KALASKADESEMILLEY** 2 b c Myboycharlie (IRE) - Congressional (IRE) (Grand Lodge (USA))
093 **KHAAWY** (USA) 2 b br f Arch (USA) - Jaleela (USA) (Kingmambo (USA))
094 **LADY IN BLUE** (IRE) 2 ch f Iffraaj - Compton Girl (Compton Place)
095 **LAUGHING DOVE** (IRE) 2 b f Tamayuz - Asfurah (USA) (Dayjur (USA))
096 **LAW KEEPER** (IRE) 2 b f Lawman (FR) - Lisieux Orchid (IRE) (Sadler's Wells (USA))
097 **LILLY JUNIOR** 2 b f Cape Cross (IRE) - Sweet Lilly (Tobougg (IRE))
098 **MANGE ALL** 2 b g Zamindar (USA) - Blancmange (Montjeu (IRE))
099 **MEETING WATERS** 2 ch f Aqlaam - Paradise Isle (Bahamian Bounty)
100 **MITRAAD** (IRE) 2 ch g Aqlaam - Badweia (USA) (Kingmambo (USA))
101 **MOCACHA** (IRE) 2 b g Camacho - Mama Angela (IRE) (Titus Livius (FR))
102 **MR MCLAREN** 2 b c Royal Applause - Mamma Morton (IRE) (Elnadim (USA))
103 **MUTAKAYYEF** 2 ch c Sea The Stars (IRE) - Infallible (Pivotal)

104 **MY INSPIRATION** (IRE) 2 b f Invincible Spirit (IRE) - Lulua (USA) (Bahri (USA))
105 **MY SPIRIT** (IRE) 2 b f Invincible Spirit (IRE) - My Renee (USA) (Kris S (USA))
106 **NEZAR** (IRE) 2 ch g Mastercraftsman (IRE) - Teddy Bears Picnic (Oasis Dream)
107 **NOTEBOOK** 2 b c Invincible Spirit (IRE) - Love Everlasting (Pursuit of Love)
108 **OUR CHANNEL** (USA) 2 ch c English Channel (USA) - Raw Gold (USA) (Rahy (USA))
109 **OXSANA** 2 b f Dubawi (IRE) - Turning Leaf (IRE) (Last Tycoon)
110 **PERFECT LIGHT** (IRE) 2 ch f Galileo (IRE) - Beauty Bright (IRE) (Danehill (USA))
111 **PERMITTED** 2 b f Authorized (IRE) - Discerning (Darshaan)
112 **PRINCESS ROSE** 2 b f Royal Applause - Mystical Spirit (IRE) (Xaar)
113 **QUEEN OF ICE** 2 ch f Selkirk (USA) - Ice Palace (Polar Falcon (USA))
114 **REDKIRK** 2 ch c Notnowcato - Flag (Selkirk (USA))
115 **RESOLUTE** 2 b g Pivotal - Coy (IRE) (Danehill (USA))
116 **ROYAL MEZYAN** (IRE) 2 b c Royal Applause - Rice Mother (IRE) (Indian Ridge)
117 **SAAYERR** 2 b c Acclamation - Adorn (Kyllachy)
118 **SCRUTINY** 2 b c Aqlaam - Aunty Mary (Common Grounds)
119 **SEAGULL STAR** 2 b c Sea The Stars (IRE) - Dash To The Top (Montjeu (IRE))
120 **SPIRITUAL FLAME** 2 b f Invincible Spirit (IRE) - Secret Flame (Machiavellian (USA))
121 **SURVIVED** 2 b f Kyllachy - Regina (Green Desert (USA))
122 **SWEET AMAALIE** (IRE) 2 b f Royal Applause - Amalie (IRE) (Fasliyev (USA))
123 **TELMEYD** 2 b c Dutch Art - Blithe (Pivotal)
124 **THIS IS THE DAY** 2 b f Footstepsinthesand - Miss Pinkerton (Danehill (USA))
125 **TREPIDATION** 2 ch c Danehill Dancer (IRE) - Trianon (Nayef (USA))
126 **UNDRESS** (IRE) 2 ch f Dalakhani (IRE) - Dress Uniform (USA) (Red Ransom (USA))
127 **WESTERLY** 2 b f Rail Link - Humility (Polar Falcon (USA))
128 **WOJHA** (IRE) 2 ch f Pivotal - Hureya (USA) (Woodman (USA))
129 **WONDERSTRUCK** (IRE) 2 b f Sea The Stars (IRE) - Bordighera (USA) (Alysheba (USA))
130 **WRANGLER** 2 b c High Chaparral (IRE) - Tipsy Me (Selkirk (USA))
131 **YUFTEN** 2 b c Invincible Spirit (IRE) - Majestic Sakeena (IRE) (King's Best (USA))
132 **ZARAEE** (IRE) 2 b c Dubawi (IRE) - Camaret (IRE) (Danehill (USA))
133 unnamed 2 b f Cape Cross (IRE) - Avila (Ajdal (USA))
134 unnamed 2 b c Oasis Dream - Enticing (IRE) (Pivotal)
135 unnamed 2 b f Myboycharlie (IRE) - Just Dreams (Salse (USA))
136 unnamed 2 b c Cape Cross (IRE) - Skiphall (Halling (USA))
137 unnamed 2 b f Elusive City (USA) - Tiger Mist (IRE) (Galileo (IRE))

Gary Harrison

Cadland Cottage, Moulton Road, NEWMARKET, Suffolk, CB8 8DU

MOBILE: 07813 846899 **EMAIL:** gary.harrison@gazeleystud.co.uk

OLDER HORSES

001 **COALBURN** 5 ch g Captain Rio - Pusey Street Girl (Gildoran (IRE))
002 **DANESIDE** (IRE) 6 b g Danehill Dancer (IRE) - Sidecar (IRE) (Spectrum (IRE))
003 **ENRICHING** (USA) 5 ch g Lemon Drop Kid (USA) - Popozinha (USA) (Rahy (USA))
004 **ONLY YOU MAGGIE** (IRE) 6 b m Atraf - First Kiss (GER) (Night Shift (USA))
005 **SAFWAAN** 6 b g Selkirk (USA) - Kawn (Cadeaux Genereux)
006 **STAR KODIAK** (IRE) 4 b f Kodiac - Red Fanfare (First Trump)

3 YEAR OLDS

007 **DUCHESS OF GAZELEY** (IRE) 3 ch f Halling (USA) - Flying Finish (FR) (Priolo (USA))
008 **ELLEN MAY** 3 b f Rock Of Gibraltar (IRE) - Triskel (Hawk Wing (USA)
009 **FORWARD MARCH** 3 b g Beat Hollow - Cantanta (Top Ville)
010 **MERIDIUS** (IRE) 3 b c Invincible Spirit (IRE) - Eliza Acton (Shirley Heights)
011 **NOT RIGG** (USA) 3 b g Henrythenavigator (USA) - St Helens Shadow (USA) (Septieme Ciel (USA))

2 YEAR OLDS

012 **BENNSON** 2 b c Compton Place - Phantasmagoria (Fraam)
013 **EMPORIUM** 2 b f Exceed And Excel (AUS) - Australian Dreams (Magic Ring (IRE))
014 **OHIO** (IRE) 2 b f Teofilo (IRE) - Royals Special (IRE) (Caerleon (USA))
015 **OUR SHERONA** 2 b f Rock of Gibraltar (IRE) - Spia (USA) (Diesis)
016 **OYSTER** (IRE) 2 br f Diamond Green (FR) - Lost Icon (IRE) (Intikhab (USA))
017 **REMY** 2 b f Oratorio (IRE) - Kristina (Kris)
018 **SEVEN LUCKY SEVEN** 2 b c Avonbridge - Moon Bird (Primo Dominie)
019 **THREE QUID** (IRE) 2 b f Clodovil (IRE) - Justice System (USA) (Criminal Type (USA))
020 **WILL** 2 ch c Kyllachy - Stormy Monday (Cadeaux Genereux)
021 unnamed 2 f Camacho - Laylati (IRE) (Green Desert (USA))
022 unnamed 2 f Kodiac - Cayambe (IRE) (Selkirk (USA))

Sarah Humphrey

Yen Hall Farm, West Wratting, Cambridge CB21 5LP

MOBILE: 07798 702484

OLDER HORSES

001 **ARFUR DIDIT** (IRE) 5 B G BLUEPRINT (IRE) - AUTHENTIC PREACHER (IRE) (BENEFICIAL)
002 **BALLY RONE** (IRE) 5 BR G FRUITS OF LOVE (USA) - PRESENTING MARBLE (IRE) (PRESENTING)
003 **BALLYHEIGUE BAY** (IRE) 6 B G RUDIMENTARY (USA) - TERINKA (IRE) (ERINS ISLE)
004 **BUZZARD FLIGHT** 4 B G KAYF TARA - IM BUSY (BUSY FLIGHT)
005 **CALL AT MIDNIGHT** 8 B M MIDNIGHT LEGEND - SECOND CALL (KIND OF HUSH)
006 **CALL HIM SOMETHING** (IRE) 5 B G HERON ISLAND - STONED IMMACULATE (IRE) (DURGAM)
007 **CARPINCHO** (FR) 9 BR G JIMBLE (FR) - LA RAPAILLE (IRE) (MANDALUS)
008 **CHAIN OF EVENTS** 6 CH G NAYEF (USA) - ERMINE (IRE) (CADEAUX GENEREUX)
009 **CHENDIYR** (FR) 4 GR G RED RANSOM (USA) - CHERRYXMA (FR) (LINAMIX)
010 **FLEMI TWO SHOES** (IRE) 7 B G FLEMENSFIRTH (USA) - SILVA VENTURE (IRE) (MANDALUS)
011 **I'M A JOKER** 4 CH G ERHAAB (USA) - YOTA (FR) (GALLETTO)
012 **I NEED A HERO** (IRE) 8 B G OSCAR SCHINDLER (IRE) - OLD FONTAINE (IRE) (MILLFONTAINE)
013 **LITTLE BIT LIVELY** (IRE) 4 GR B FLEMENSFIRTH (USA) - MIRANDA'S LACE (IRE) (BACH)
014 **MINELLA HERO** (IRE) 5 B G OLD VIC - SHANNON ROSE (IRE) (TOPANOORA)
015 **MOYALIFF** (IRE) 6 BR G KING'S THEATRE (IRE) - INSTANT QUEEN (IRE) (EXECUTIVE PERK)
016 **PRESENTING PADDY** (IRE) 5 B G PRESENTING - BULA BEAG (IRE) (BRUSH ASIDE)
017 **TORNADE D'ESTRUVAL** (FR) 6 BR M NETWORK (GER) - ONDE D'ESTRUVAL (FR) (ART BLEU)
018 **VASCO D'YCY** (FR) 4 BR G EQUERRY (USA) - INGRID DES MOTTES (FR) (USEFUL)

Alison Hutchinson

Paddocks Yard, Exeter Stables, Church Street, Exning CB8 7EH
Correspondence to: 116 Parkers Walk, Studlands, Newmarket CB8 7AP

TEL: 01638 610030 **MOBILE:** 07960 630204

OLDER HORSES

001 **BIG WAVE** (IRE) 5 b m Choisir (AUS) - Mystery Solved (USA) (Royal Academy (USA))
002 **ICEMAN GEORGE** 9 b g Beat Hollow - Diebiedale (Dominion)
003 **MUCKY MOLLY** 5 ch m Bahamian Bounty - Indian Flag (IRE) (Indian Ridge)
004 **STRIKE FORCE** 9 b g Dansili - Miswaki Belle (USA) (Miswaki (USA))

William Jarvis

Phantom House, Fordham Road, Newmarket, Suffolk CB8 7AA

Tel: 01638 669873 / 662677 (h) **Fax:** 01638 667328 **Mobile:** 07836 261884

OLDER HORSES

001 **ASHDOWN LAD** 4 ch g Sir Percy - Antibes (IRE) (Grand Lodge (USA))
002 **BEAUFORT TWELVE** 4 b g Hurricane Run (IRE) - Violette (Observatory (USA))
003 **CARAZAM** (IRE) 6 b g Azamour (IRE) - Carallia (IRE) (Common Grounds)
004 **DIXIE'S DREAM** (IRE) 4 b c Hawk Wing (USA) - Hams (USA) (Dixie Union (USA))
005 **EMBANKMENT** 4 b c Zamindar (USA) - Esplanade (Danehill (USA))
006 **KATY'S SECRET** 6 b m Mind Games - Katy O'Hara (Komaite (USA))
007 **LOKI'S REVENGE** 5 b g Kyllachy - Amira (Efisio)
008 **PRIVATE EQUITY** (IRE) 7 b m Haafhd - Profit Alert (IRE) (Alzao (USA))

3 YEAR OLDS

009 **ARGENT KNIGHT** 3 gr g Sir Percy - Tussah (Daylami (IRE))
010 **BOSHAM** 3 b c Shamardal (USA) - Awwal Malika (USA) (Kingmambo (USA))
011 **CAVALIERI** (IRE) 3 b c Oratorio (IRE) - Always Attractive (IRE) (King's Best (USA))
012 **CRAVE** 3 b f Sakhee's Secret - Bolsena (USA) (Red Ransom (USA))
013 **DUMBARTON ROCK** 3 b g Kyllachy - Ellablue (Bahamian Bounty)
014 **EL MASSIVO** (IRE) 3 b c Authorized (IRE) - Umthoulah (IRE) (Unfuwain (USA))
015 **JODIES JEM** 3 br g Kheleyf (USA) - First Approval (Royal Applause)
016 **LAUDATION** 3 b c Royal Applause - Calamanco (Clantime)
017 **NIGHT'S WATCH** 3 b c Authorized (IRE) - Nachtigall (GER) (Danehill (USA))
018 **PERSIAN PATRIOT** 3 ch f Bahamian Bounty - Persian Lass (IRE) (Grand Lodge (USA))
019 **RASKOVA** (USA) 3 b f Henrythenavigator (USA) - Diamond Necklace (USA) (Unbridled's Song (USA))

2 YEAR OLDS

020 **AMETRINE** (IRE) 2 b f Fastnet Rock (AUS) - Amethyst (IRE) (Sadler's Wells (USA))
021 **BEAKERS N NUM NUMS** (IRE) 2 b c Iffraaj - Ivy League Star (IRE) (Sadler's Wells (USA))
022 **BISHAN BEDI** (IRE) 2 b c Intikhab (USA) - Knockatotaun (Spectrum (IRE))
023 **BLURRED VISION** 2 b c Royal Applause - Sparkling Eyes (Lujain (USA))
024 **HALLAGA** 2 ch f Halling (USA) - Gayanula (USA) (Yonaguska (USA))
025 **NEW ROW** 2 b f Teofilo (IRE) - Memo (Groom Dancer (USA))
026 **SILVER MOUNTAIN** 2 gr c Sir Percy - Pearl Bright (FR) (Kaldoun (FR))
027 unnamed 2 b f Dubawi (IRE) - Bronwen (IRE) (King's Best (USA))

Tommy Keddy

Southgate Stables, Hamilton Road, Newmarket CB8 0WY
Correspondence to 246 Exning Road, Newmarket CB8 0AN

Tel: 01638 561498 **Mobile:** 07542 036544 **Mobile:** 07745 238018 **Fax:** 01638 561498

NO HORSE LIST AVAILABLE AT TIME OF GOING TO PRESS

Miss Gay Kelleway

Queen Alexandra Stables, Chapel Street, Exning, Newmarket, Suffolk CB8 7HA

Fax: 01638 577778 **Mobile:** 07974 948768

OLDER HORSES

001 **CONDUCTING** 5 b g Oratorio (IRE) - Aiming (Highest Honor (FR))
002 **LAYLINE** (IRE) 6 b g King's Best (USA) - Belle Reine (King of Kings (IRE))
003 **SWING ALONE** (IRE) 4 b g Celtic Swing - Groupetime (USA) (Gilded Time (USA))
004 **YOJOJO** (IRE) 4 ch f Windsor Knot (IRE) - Belle of The Blues (IRE) (Blues Traveller (IRE))

3 YEAR OLDS

005 **DESTINY HIGHWAY** (FR) 3 b g Sir Percy - Grace Bankes (Efisio)
006 **ERIN'S GRACE** (IRE) 3 b f Tagula (IRE) - Crystal Theatre (IRE) (King's Theatre (IRE))
007 **HOLY WARRIOR** (IRE) 3 b c Holy Roman Emperor (IRE) - If Dubai (USA) (Stephen Got Even (USA))
008 **PIXILATED** 3 b g Phoenix Reach (IRE) - Chocolada (Namid)
009 **PRAIRIE PRINCE** (IRE) 3 b g High Chaparral (IRE) - Palatine Dancer (IRE) (Namid)
010 **SMILESWITHHISEYES** (IRE) 3 b g Marju (IRE) - Amoureux (USA) (Deputy Minister (CAN))
011 **SPANISH ART** 3 b g Byron - Spanish Gold (Vettori (IRE))
012 **TRIPLE AITCH** (USA) 3 b c Harlan's Holiday (USA) - Hadley (USA) (Kingmambo (USA))

2 YEAR OLDS

013 **AUSTERIAN** 2 ro c Mastercraftsman (IRE) - Singed (Zamindar (USA))
014 **CHANCEUSE** 2 b f Lucky Story (USA) - Miss Madame (IRE) (Cape Cross (IRE))
015 **DANZKI** (IRE) 2 b c Bushranger (IRE) - Miniver (IRE) (Mujtahid (USA))
016 **LUCKY SURPRISE** 2 b f Lucky Story (USA) - Bella Bertolini (Bertolini (USA))
017 **LUCKY VISIONE** 2 b c Lucky Story (USA) - Maid For Running (Namaqualand (USA))
018 **MIZZENI** (FR) 2 gr c Verglas (IRE) - Bashful (IRE) (Brief Truce (USA))
019 **SEALED** (USA) 2 b br c Speightstown (USA) - Sinister Sister (USA) (Formal Dinner (USA))
020 **SOUL OF MOTION** 2 b c Phoenix Reach (IRE) - Chocolada (Namid)

Neil King

St Gatien Racing, St Gatien Cottage, Vicarage Road, Newmarket, Suffolk CB8 8HP

Tel: 01638 666150 **Fax:** 01638 666150 **Mobile:** 07880 702325

OLDER HORSES

001 **ATTWAAL** (IRE) 4 b g Teofilo (IRE) - Qasirah (IRE) (Machiavellian (USA))
002 **BALLYVONEEN** (IRE) 8 b g Stowaway - Miss Ira Zarad (IRE) (Darazari (IRE))
003 **BOLLIN TAHINI** 7 b m Bollin Eric - Cinnamon Club (Derrylin)
004 **CERIUM** (FR) 12 b g Vaguely Pleasant (FR) - Tantatura (FR) (Akarad (FR))
005 **DELGANY GUNNER** 9 b g Commanche Run - No Grandad (Strong Gale)
006 **EVELLA** (IRE) 9 ch m Beneficial - Drimadrian (Gildoran)
007 **GET READY TO GO** (IRE) 9 b g Turtle Island (IRE) - Buckalong (IRE) (Buckskin (FR))
008 **KAYSERSBERG** (FR) 6 b g Khalkevi (IRE) - Alliance Royale (FR) (Turgeon (USA))
009 **KELTIC RHYTHM** (IRE) 6 b g Milan - Ballinaroone Girl (IRE) (Carroll House)
010 **MAXILIAN** (IRE) 4 b g Milan - Super Size (IRE) (Shernazar)
011 **NATIVE COLONY** 5 b g St Jovite (USA) - Self Esteem (Suave Dancer (USA))
012 **ONTHESLATE** (IRE) 7 b g Beneficial - Florida (IRE) (Sri Pekan (USA))
013 **OUTBACK** (IRE) 4 b g Kodiac - Florida City (IRE) (Pennekamp (USA))
014 **PAIRC NA GCAPALL** (IRE) 11 b g Taipan (IRE) - Ballindante (IRE) (Phardante (FR))
015 **PEINTRE STER** (IRE) 6 ch g Peintre Celebre (USA) - Goldster (IRE) (Intikhab (USA))
016 **PERSIAN HERALD** 5 gr g Proclamation (IRE) - Persian Fortune (Forzando)
017 **SAMARKAND** (IRE) 5 b g Sadler's Wells (USA) - Romantic Venture (IRE) (Indian Ridge)
018 **WOM** 5 b g Tiger Hill (IRE) - Vayavaig (Damister (USA))
019 **ZEROESHADESOFGREY** (IRE) 4 gr g Portrait Gallery (IRE) - Hazy Rose (IRE) (Roselier (FR))

Cliff Lines

Hethersett House, Church Street, Exning, Newmarket, Suffolk, CB8 7EH

Tel / Fax : 01638 608016 Mobile : 07980 120157

OLDER HORSES

001 **AARANYOW** (IRE) 5 ch g Compton Place - Cutpurse Moll (Green Desert (USA))
002 **PROUD CHIEFTAIN** 5 b g Sleeping Indian - Skimra (Hernando (FR))

Nick Littmoden

Brook Farm, Dullingham Ley, Newmarket CB8 9XG

Tel: 01638 508491 **Fax:** 01638 661948 **Mobile:** 07770 964865

NO HORSE LIST AVAILABLE AT TIME OF GOING TO PRESS

George G Margarson

Graham Lodge, Birdcage Walk, Newmarket, Suffolk CB8 0NF

Tel: 01638 668043 **Fax:** 01638 668043 **Mobile:** 07860 198303

OLDER HORSES

001 **ARTFUL LADY** (IRE) 4 br f Excellent Art - Fear And Greed (IRE) (Brief Truce (USA))
002 **EXCELLENT AIM** 6 b g Exceed And Excel (AUS) - Snugfit Annie (Midyan (USA))
003 **EXCELLENT GUEST** 6 b g Exceed And Excel (AUS) - Princess Speedfit (FR) (Desert Prince (IRE))
004 **IMAGINARY DIVA** 7 b m Lend A Hand - Distant Diva (Distant Relative)
005 **MAGICAL SPEEDFIT** (IRE) 8 ch g Bold Fact (USA) - Magical Peace (IRE) (Magical Wonder (USA))
006 **REBELLIOUS GUEST** 4 b g Cockney Rebel (IRE) - Marisa (GER) (Desert Sun)
007 **STORM RUNNER** (IRE) 5 b g Rakti - Saibhreas (IRE) (Last Tycoon)
008 **UPRISE** 4 b g Pivotal - Soar (Danzero (AUS))
009 **WOOLFALL SOVEREIGN** (IRE) 7 b g Noverre (USA) - Mandragore (USA) (Slew O' Gold (USA))
010 **YOUNG JACKIE** 5 b m Doyen (IRE) - Just Warning (Warning)
011 **YOUNG LISA** 4 b f Echo of Light - Just Warning (Warning)

3 YEAR OLDS

012 **EXOTIC GUEST** 3 ch g Bahamian Bounty - Mamoura (IRE) (Lomond (USA))
013 **JAMMY GUEST** (IRE) 3 b c Duke of Marmalade (IRE) - Ardbrae Lady (Overbury (IRE))
014 **RED CATKIN** 3 b f Notnowcato - Red Salvia (Selkirk (USA))
015 **SPEEDFIT BOY** (IRE) 3 b g Red Clubs (IRE) - Princess Speedfit (FR) (Desert Prince (IRE))

2 YEAR OLDS

016 **BOUNTIFUL SIN** 2 ch c Sinndar (IRE) - Tropical Barth (IRE) (Peintre Celebre (USA))
017 **ELUSIVE GUEST** (FR) 2 b c Elusive City (USA) - Mansoura (IRE) (Kalanisi (IRE))
018 **JAY GEE SPEEDFIT** (IRE) 2 b c Bushranger (IRE) - Prodigal Daughter (Alhaarth (IRE))
019 **LUCKY KRISTALE** 2 b f Lucky Story (USA) - Pikaboo (Pivotal)
020 **SHYRON** 2 b c Byron - Coconut Shy (Bahamian Bounty)

P J (Charlie) McBride

Exeter House Stables, Exeter Road, Newmarket CB8 8LP

Tel: 01638 667841 **Fax:** 01638 667841 **Mobile:** 07929 265711

OLDER HORSES

001 **AMOYA** (GER) 6 b m Royal Dragon (USA) - Arkona (GER) (Aspros (GER))
002 **BANK ON ME** 4 ch g Medicean - Red Garland (Selkirk (USA))
003 **HARRY BUCKLE** 4 ch g Byron - Native Ring (FR) (Bering)
004 **PORCINI** 4 b f Azamour (IRE) - Portal (Hernando (FR))

3 YEAR OLDS

005 **KEENE** 3 b g Cockney Rebel (IRE) - Lumpini Park (Halling (USA))
006 **NAPINDA** 3 b f Sleeping Indian - Aptina (USA) (Aptitude (USA))
007 **SUPER COOKIE** 3 b f Dylan Thomas (IRE) - Dance Lesson (In The Wings)

2 YEAR OLDS

008 **BLUE OYSTER** 2 b f Medicean - Bluebelle (Generous (IRE))
009 **BRIGLIADORO** (IRE) 2 ch c Excellent Art - Milady's Pride (Machiavellian (USA))
010 **ONE PENNY PIECE** 2 b f Archipenko (USA) - Silken Promise (USA) (Pulpit (USA))
011 **RAZOR QUEST** 2 b c Virtual - Takarna (IRE) (Mark of Esteem (IRE))

Phil McEntee

Racefield Stables, formerly Carriageway Stables, Hamilton Road, Newmarket CB8 7JQ

Mobile Phone 07802 663256 **Work Phone** 01638 668806 **Fax** 01638 662092
Email mcentee6@btinternet.com

OLDER HORSES

001 **BACK FOR TEA** (IRE) 5 b g Redback - Jasmine Pearl (IRE) (King of Kings (IRE))
002 **BIRD DOG** 7 ch g Compton Place - Form At Last (Formidable (USA))
003 **ISHIAMIRACLE** 4 ch f Ishiguru (USA) - Sukuma (IRE) (Highest Honor (FR))
004 **JONNIE SKULL** (IRE) 7 b g Pyrus (USA) - Sovereign Touch (IRE) (Pennine Walk)
005 **KING OF WING** (IRE) 4 b g Hawk Wing (USA) - Miss Shivvy (IRE) (Montjeu (IRE))
006 **PUTIN** (IRE) 5 b g Fasliyev (USA) - Consignia (IRE) (Definite Article)
007 **SILK SKY** 7 ch m Shahrastani (USA) - Insulate (Sula Bula)
008 **SWISS CROSS** 6 b g Cape Cross (IRE) - Swiss Lake (USA) (Indian Ridge)
009 **THE BLUE DOG** (IRE) 6 b m High Chaparral (IRE) - Jules (IRE) (Danehill (USA))
010 **THOUGHTSOFSTARDOM** 10 b g Mind Games - Alustar (Emarati (USA))

3 YEAR OLDS

011 **LILLY MAY** (IRE) 3 b f Haatef (USA) - Love of Silver (USA) (Arctic Tern (USA))
012 **MINIMEE** 3 b g Dubai Destination (USA) - Malaaq (Green Desert (USA))
013 **TWO NO BIDS** (IRE) 3 b br g Footstepsinthesand - Milwaukee (FR) (Desert King (IRE))

2 YEAR OLDS

014 **BAYTOWN KESTREL** 2 b f Captain Gerrard (IRE) - Litewska (IRE) (Mujadil (USA))
015 **FLYING AUTHOR** (IRE) 2 b c Authorized (IRE) - Fly Free (Halling (USA))

Ismail Mohammed

Revida Place Stables, Hamilton Road, Newmarket, Suffolk, CB8 7JQ

Tel: 01638 669074 **Mobile:** 07771 777121 **Office:** 07775 772524 (sec)

OLDER HORSES

001 **ADMIRALTY** 4 b c Iffraaj - Camp Riverside (USA) (Forest Camp (USA))
002 **AUTUMNUS** (IRE) 4 b g Manduro (GER) - Turning Light (GER) (Fantastic Light (USA))
003 **CAPE SAMBA** 4 b g Cape Cross (IRE) - Dancing Feather (Suave Dancer (USA))
004 **COMETOGRAPHY** (IRE) 4 b c Teofilo (IRE) - Halle Bop (Dubai Millennium)
005 **EDUCATE** 4 b g Echo of Light - Pasithea (IRE) (Celtic Swing)
006 **LIGHT BURST** (USA) 4 b c Hard Spun (USA) - Kew Garden (USA) (Seattle Slew (USA))
007 **MUBTADI** 5 b g Dr Fong (USA) - Noble Peregrine (Lomond (USA))
008 **SHAMAAL NIBRAS** (USA) 4 b c First Samurai (USA) - Sashay Away (USA) (Farma Way (USA))

3 YEAR OLDS

009 **ALHAARTH BEAUTY** (IRE) 3 b f Alhaarth (IRE) - Endis (IRE) (Distant Relative)
010 **ANA SHABABIYA** (IRE) 3 ch f Teofilo (IRE) - Call Later (USA) (Gone West (USA))
011 **COURT LIFE** (IRE) 3 ch c New Approach (IRE) - Tudor Court (IRE) (Cape Cross (IRE))
012 **MAGIC LANDO** (FR) 3 b c Lando (GER) - Blackberry Pie (USA) (Gulch (USA))
013 **RED WARRIOR** (IRE) 3 ch c Iffraaj - Wiolante (GER) (Lagunas)
014 **RHOMBUS** (IRE) 3 b g Authorized (IRE) - Mathool (IRE) (Alhaarth (IRE))

2 YEAR OLDS

015 **DUBAWI FUN** 2 b c Dubawi (IRE) - Arabian Treasure (USA) (Danzig (USA))
016 **MOTAMAYEZAH** 2 ch f Tamayuz - Classical Dancer (Dr Fong (USA))
017 **STORMARDAL** (IRE) 2 b c Shamardal (USA) - Dievotchkina (IRE) (Bluebird (USA))
018 unnamed 2 b c New Approach (IRE) - Al Hasnaa (Zafonic (USA))
019 unnamed 2 ch f New Approach (IRE) - Dance Treat (USA) (Nureyev (USA))
020 unnamed 2 b c Iffraaj - Tortue (IRE) (Turtle Island (IRE))
021 unnamed 2 b c Nayef (USA) - Voile (IRE) (Barathea (IRE))

Kevin Morgan

Gazeley Park Stables, 15 Moulton Road, Gazeley, Newmarket CB8 8RA

Tel/Fax: 01638 551888 **Mobile:** 07768 996103

NO HORSE LIST AVAILABLE AT TIME OF GOING TO PRESS

David Morris

Beverley House Stables (Second Yard), Exeter Road, Newmarket CB8 8LR
Correspondence to Mokefield, Baxters Green, Wickhambrook, Newmarket CB8 8UY

Tel: 01284 850348- **Mobile:** 07711 010268

NO HORSE LIST AVAILABLE AT TIME OF GOING TO PRESS

Michael Murphy

Cedar Lodge Stables, Hamilton Rd, Newmarket CB8 0NQ
Correspondence: 76 Weston Way, Newmarket CB8 7SF

Tel: 01638 561099- **Mobile:** 07951 766035

OLDER HORSES

001 **CELTIC LEGACY** 6 ch m Where Or When (IRE) - An Cailin Rua (Aragon)
002 **EDIN BURGHER** (FR) 12 br g Hamas (IRE) - Jaljuli (Jalmood (USA))
003 **ENTHUSIASTIC** 5 b h Galileo (IRE) - Que Puntual (ARG) (Contested Bid (USA))
004 **JACK FIREFLY** 4 b g Echo of Light - Charlottebutterfly (Millkom)
005 **LAW HILL** 4 b c Zamindar (USA) - Absoluta (IRE) (Royal Academy (USA))
006 **NOGUCHI** (IRE) 8 ch g Pivotal - Tuscania (USA) (Woodman (USA))
007 **ROCK OF AGES** 4 ch g Pivotal - Magic Peak (IRE) (Danehill (USA))

2 YEAR OLDS

008 **BOURBONDI** 2 b c Sakhee (USA) - Lake Diva (Docksider (USA))

William J Musson

Saville House, St Mary's Square, Newmarket, Suffolk CB8 0HZ

Tel: 01638 663371 **Fax:** 01638 667979.

OLDER HORSES

001 **ABSOLUTELY ME** (IRE) 4 ch f Barathea (IRE) - Attymon Lill (IRE) (Marju (IRE))
002 **AKARANA** (IRE) 6 b g Danehill Dancer (IRE) - Castle Quest (IRE) (Grand Lodge (USA))
003 **BOLD ADVENTURE** 9 ch g Arkadian Hero (USA) - Impatiente (USA) (Vaguely Noble)
004 **BROUGHTONS BANDIT** 6 b g Kyllachy - Broughton Bounty (Bahamian Bounty)
005 **BROUGHTONS STAR** 6 ch g Starcraft (NZ) - Marrakech (IRE) (Barathea (IRE))
006 **CAPRISKA** 4 b f Bahri (USA) - Guignol (IRE) (Anita's Prince)
007 **COMMON TOUCH** (IRE) 5 ch g Compton Place - Flying Finish (FR) (Priolo (USA))
008 **COZY TIGER** (USA) 8 gr g Hold That Tiger (USA) - Cozelia (USA) (Cozzene (USA))
009 **EMEEBEE** 7 b g Medicean - Broughtons Motto (Mtoto)
010 **MAC'S POWER** (IRE) 7 b g Exceed And Excel (AUS) - Easter Girl (Efisio)
011 **MOUNTAIN RANGE** (IRE) 5 b g High Chaparral (IRE) - Tuscany Lady (IRE) (Danetime (IRE))
012 **NOVELLEN LAD** (IRE) 8 b g Noverre (USA) - Lady Ellen (Horage)
013 **ROCKET ROB** (IRE) 7 b g Danetime (IRE) - Queen of Fibres (IRE) (Scenic)
014 **RUSTIC DEACON** 6 ch g Pastoral Pursuits - Anne-Lise (Inchinor)
015 unnamed 4 b g Araafa (IRE) - Broughton Singer (IRE) (Common Grounds)

3 YEAR OLDS

016 **BROUGHTONS CHARM** (IRE) 3 b f Invincible Spirit (IRE) - Parisian Elegance (Zilzal (USA))
017 unnamed 3 ch g Byron - Hetra Heights (USA) (Cox's Ridge (USA))

2 YEAR OLDS

018 **BROUGHTONS SECRET** 2 b f Aqlaam - Hidden Meaning (Cadeaux Genereux)
019 **DONT HAVE IT THEN** 2 b c Myboycharlie (IRE) - Mondovi (Kyllachy)
020 unnamed 2 b c Medicean - Lifetime Romance (IRE) (Mozart (IRE))
021 unnamed 2 b c Dandy Man (IRE) - Ribald (Alhaarth (IRE))

Jeremy Noseda

Shalfleet Stables, Bury Road, Newmarket, Suffolk CB8 7BX

Tel: 01638 664010 **Mobile:** 07710 294093 **Fax:** 01638 664010 **Email:** jeremy noseda@virgin.net

OLDER HORSES

001 **PETER MARTINS** (USA) 5 ch g Johannesburg (USA)-Pretty Meadow (USA(Meadowlake)
002 **LYRIC STREET** (IRE) 5 b g Hurricane Run (IRE)-Elle Danzig (GER) (Roi Danzig)
003 **INSTANCE** (GB) 5 b m Invincible Spirit (IRE)-Hannda (IRE) (Dr Devious)
004 **GRANDEUR** (IRE) 4 gr g Verglas (IRE)-Misskinta (IRE) (Desert Sun)
005 **HARVARD N YALE** (USA) 4 ch c Smart Strike (CAN)-Compete (USA) (El Prado)
006 **NET WHIZZ** (USA) 4 dkb/br c Mr Greeley (USA)-Reboot (USA) (Rubiano)
007 **VALBCHEK** (IRE) 4 b g Acclamation-Spectacular Show (IRE) (Spectrum)
008 **NOCTURN** (GB) 4 b g Oasis Dream- Pizzicato (Statoblest)
009 **BURKE'S ROCK** (GB) 4 br f Cape Cross (IRE)-Miss Lacey (IRE) (Diktat)
010 **RECKONING** (IRE) 4 b f Danehill Dancer (IRE)-Great Hope (IRE) (Halling)

3 YEAR OLDS

011 **ACHTUNG** (GB) 3 b c Montjeu (IRE)-Funsie (FR) (Saumarez)
012 **CONSIGN** (GB) 3 b g Dutch Art-Maid to Dance (Pyramus)
013 **DUTIFUL SON** (IRE) 3 b c Invincible Spirit (IRE)-Grecian Dancer (Dansili)
014 **EVIDENT** (IRE) 3 b c Excellent Art-Vestavia (IRE) (Alhaarth)
015 **EXCUSE TO LINGER** (GB) 3 ch c Compton Place-Lady Le Quesne (IRE) (Alhaarth)
016 **FANTASTIC MOON** (GB) 3 ch c Dalakhani (IRE)-Rhadegunda (Pivotal)
017 **HI FILWAH** (USA) 3 b c Medaglia d'Oro (USA)-Star Landing (USA) (Caller I D)
018 **HOMAGE** (IRE) 3 b c Acclamation-Night Sphere (IRE) (Night Shift)
019 **HORNBOY** (GB) 3 b g Medicean-Soar (Danzero)
020 **IAN'S DREAM** (USA) 3 ch c Speightstown (USA)-She's Loaded (USA) (Deputy Minister)
021 **INTIMIDATE** (GB) 3 b c Royal Applause-Crystal Power (USA) (Pleasant Colony)
022 **INTREPID** (IRE) 3 b g Invincible Spirit (IRE)-Imiloa (USA) (Kingmambo)
023 **INVESTMENT EXPERT** (IRE) 3 b g Tamayuz-Kindling (Dr Fong)
024 **JOE PALOOKA** (IRE) 3 b c Galileo (IRE)-Glinting Desert (IRE) (Desert Prince)
025 **MESSILA STAR** (GB) 3 ch c Pivotal-Jamboretta (IRE) (Danehill)
026 **OCEAN SECRET** (IRE) 3 ch c Shirocco (GER)-Shell Garland (USA) (Sadler's Wells)
027 **PROPHETS PRIDE** (GB) 3 b c Sakhee (USA)-Winner's Call (Indian Ridge)
028 **SILVER DIXIE** (USA) 3 b c Dixie Union (USA)- More Silver (USA) (Silver Hawk)
029 **SWEET DEAL** (IRE) 3 gr g Verglas (IRE)-Compromise (FR) (Fasliyev)
030 **THE BEST DOCTOR** (IRE) 3 ch c Pivotal-Strawberry Fledge (USA) (Kingmambo)
031 **WAR HORSE** (GB) 3 b c Galileo (IRE)-Distinctive Look (IRE) (Danehill)
032 **WARRIGAL** (IRE) 3 ch c Mount Nelson-Waldblume (GER) (Halling)
033 **YEAGER** (USA) 3 b/br c Medaglia d'Oro (USA)-Lucky Flyer (USA) (Fusaichi Pegasus)
034 **ZAMOYSKI** (GB) 3 ch g Dutch Art-Speech (Red Ransom)
035 **ARCADIAN LEGEND** (USA) 3 b f Van Nistelrooy (USA)-Miss Zafonic (FR) (Zafonic)
036 **COCONELL** (GB) 3 b f Rock of Gibraltar (IRE)-Marula (IRE) (Sadler's Wells)
037 **ELAS LAW** (GB) 3 gr f Lawman (FR)-Ela Athena (Ezzoud)
038 **ENDLESS LIGHT** (GB) 3 ch f Pivotal-Celeste (Green Desert)
039 **EXEMPT** (GB) 3 gr f Exceed and Excel (AUS)-Miss University (USA) (Beau Genius)
040 **HAVELOVEWILLTRAVEL** (IRE) 3 dk b Holy Roman Emperor (IRE)-Strategy (Machiavellian)
041 **GREEK SPIRIT** (IRE) 3 b f Invincible Spirit (IRE)-Greek Symphony (IRE) (Mozart)
042 **KEPT WELL** (USA) 3 b f Scat Daddy (USA)-Prosperous Move (USA) (Arch)
043 **MAGIQUE** (IRE) 3 b f Jeremy (USA)-Misskinta (IRE) (Desert Sun)
044 **MARIA LOMBARDI** (GB) 3 b f Medicean-Fabulously Fast (USA) (Deputy Minister)
045 **RED BATON** (GB) 3 b f Exceed and Excel (AUS)-Ruby Rocket (IRE) (Indian Rocket)
046 **REGAL SILK** (GB) 3 b f Pivotal-Regal Velvet (Halling)
047 **RED TURBAN** (GB) 3 b f Kyllachy-Red Tiara (USA) (Mr Prospector)
048 **THE GOLD CHEONGSAM** (IRE) 3 b f Red Clubs (IRE)-Fuerta Ventura (IRE) (Desert Sun)

2 YEAR OLDS

049 **ANAKAYA** (GB) 2 b c Pastoral Pursuits-Rhapsilian (Dansili)
050 **BISHOPS AVENUE** (IRE) 2 b c Lawman (FR)- Shesasmartlady (IRE) (Dolphin Street)
051 **DANCE OF HEROES** (GB) 2 b c Danehill Dancer (IRE)-Helena Molony (IRE) (Sadler's Wells)
052 **DRACO'S CODE** (GB) 2 b c Galileo (IRE)-Lady Karr (Mark Of Esteem)
053 **GONE WITH THE WIND** (GER) 2 b c Dutch Art-Gallivant (Danehill)
054 **IAN'S MEMORY** (USA) 2 dk b / br c Smart Strike (CAN)-Rite Moment (USA) (Vicar)
055 **JOHN CAESAR** (IRE) 2 b c Bushranger (IRE)-Polish Belle (Polish Precedent)
056 **KAGAMI** (GB) 2 ch c Teofilo (IRE)-Sky Wonder (Observatory)
057 **OUTBACK TRAVELLER** (IRE) 2 b c Bushranger (IRE)- Blue Holly (IRE) (Blues Traveller)
058 **NIGEL'S DESTINY** (USA) 2 b c Giant's Causeway (USA)-Ticket To Seattle (USA) (Capote)
059 **REGAL SASH** (GB) 2 br c Pivotal-Regal Riband (Fantastic Light)
060 **ROMAN LEGEND** (IRE) 2 b c Holy Roman Emperor (IRE)-Taking Liberties (IRE) (Royal Academy)
061 **YELLOW EMPEROR** (IRE) 2 b c Holy Roman Emperor (IRE)-Valentine Hill (IRE) (Mujadil)
062 **ZESHOV** (IRE) 2 b c Acclamation-Fathoming (USA) (Gulch)
063 **ANNA'S FANCY** (IRE) 2 gr f Acclamation-StepToo Far (USA) (Cozzene)
064 **ANNA'S VISION** (IRE) 2 b f Invincible Spirit (IRE)-House In Wood (FR) (Woodman)
065 **AUTUMNS BLUSH** (IRE) 2 b f Kheleyf (USA)-Park Romance (IRE) (Dr Fong)
066 **BIJOU BLANCHE** (GB) 2 b f Azamour(IRE)-Shanghai Lily IRE) (King's Best)
067 **DREAMING BEAUTY** (GB) 2 b f Oasis Dream-Independence (Selkirk)
068 **EXPECT** (GB) 2 b f Invincible Spirit (IRE) – Expressive (Falbrav)
069 **HEAVENLY** (GB) 2 ch f Pivotal-Celeste (Green Desert)
070 **MARGARET'S MISSION** (IRE) 2 b f Shamardal (USA)-Wimple (Kingmambo)
071 **MERLETTA** (GB) 2 b f Raven's Pass (USA)-Light Hearted (Green Desert)
072 **NIGHTLIGHT** (GB) 2 b f Pivotal-Floodlit (Fantastic Light)
073 **RED VELOUR** (GB) 2 ch f Pivotal-Regal Velvet (Halling)
074 **SHAMA'S CROWN** (IRE) 2 ch f New Approach (IRE)-Classic Park (Robellino)
075 **THE SILVER KEBAYA** (FR) 2 b f Rock Of Gibraltar (IRE)-Music House (IRE) (Singspiel)
076 **VIRTUALLY** (GB) 2 b f Virtual-Red Tiara (USA) (Mr Prospector)
077 **YOU'VE GOT IT** (GB) 2 b f Sea The Stars (IRE)-Song (IRE) (Sadler's Wells)
078 Unnamed 2 ch c Candy Ride (ARG) – Apt (USA) (A.P.Indy)
079 Unnamed 2 b c Henrythenavigator (USA)- Bosset (USA) (Stravinsky)
080 Unnamed 2 b c Exchange Rate (USA)-Colonna Traiana (CHI) (Roy)
081 Unnamed 2 b/gr c Duke Of Marmalade (IRE)-Exotic Mix (FR) (Linamix)
082 Unnamed 2 b c High Chaparral (IRE)-Hana Dee (Cadeaux Genereux)
083 Unnamed 2 br f More Than Ready (USA)-High Heel Sneakers (Dansili)

P J O'Gorman

Seven Springs, Hamilton Road, Newmarket, Suffolk CB8 7JQ

Tel: 01638 667070 **Mobile:** 07789 724742

NO HORSE LIST AVAILABLE AT TIME OF GOING TO PRESS

Hugo Palmer

Kremlin Cottage Stables, Snailwell Road, NEWMARKET, Suffolk, CB8 7DP

MOBILE: 07824 887886

OLDER HORSES

001 **ASCRIPTION** (IRE) 4 b c Dansili - Lady Elgar (IRE) (Sadler's Wells (USA))
002 **GAME ALL** (IRE) 4 b f Acclamation - Love Thirty (Mister Baileys)
003 **KHUBALA** (IRE) 4 b c Acclamation - Raghida (IRE) (Nordico (USA))
004 **MAKING EYES** (IRE) 5 b m Dansili - Lady's View (USA) (Distant View (USA))
005 **ZERO MONEY** (IRE) 7 ch g Bachelor Duke (USA) - Dawn Chorus (IRE) (Mukaddamah (USA))

3 YEAR OLDS

006 **AUDACIA** (IRE) 3 b f Sixties Icon - Indiannie Moon (Fraam)
007 **BORN TO RUN** 3 b f Ishiguru (USA) - Maid For Running (Namaqualand (USA))
008 **EARLY ONE MORNING** 3 b f Medicean - Still Small Voice (Polish Precedent (USA))
009 **FLAWLESS BEAUTY** 3 b f Excellent Art - Desert Classic (Green Desert (USA))
010 **HIGH TIME TOO** (IRE) 3 b f High Chaparral (IRE) - Dane Thyme (IRE) (Danetime (IRE))
011 **NURSE CELIA** 3 b f Nayef (USA) - Tincture (Dr Fong (USA))
012 **QUEENOFTHENORTH** (IRE) 3 b f Halling (USA) - Polska (USA) (Danzig (USA))
013 **RED RED WINE** 3 b c Dutch Art - Atnab (USA) (Riverman (USA))
014 **SHORT SQUEEZE** (IRE) 3 b g Cape Cross (IRE) - Sunsetter (USA) (Diesis)
015 **TIPPING OVER** (IRE) 3 gr f Aussie Rules (USA) - Precipice (Observatory (USA))
016 **TWO IN THE PINK** (IRE) 3 b f Clodovil (IRE) - Secret Circle (Magic Ring (IRE))

2 YEAR OLDS

017 **CLOSE COMPANION** 2 b f Azamour (IRE) - Vittoria Vetra (Danehill Dancer (IRE))
018 **EXTREMITY** (IRE) 2 ch c Exceed And Excel (AUS) - Chanterelle (IRE) (Indian Ridge)
019 **KNIFE POINT** (GER) 2 b c High Chaparral (IRE) - Knightsbridge (BRZ) (Yagli (USA))
020 **LOBSTER POT** 2 b f Dylan Thomas (IRE) - Classical Flair (Distant Music (USA))
021 **PHOTOGRAPHY** (IRE) 2 b c Haatef (USA) - Sierva (GER) (Darshaan)
022 **PYJAMA DAY** 2 b f Royal Applause - Miss Otis (Danetime (IRE))
023 **TACTICAL STRIKE** 2 ch c Pivotal - Alvee (IRE) (Key of Luck (USA))
024 **THREE HEART'S** 2 b f Three Valleys (USA) - Heart's Harmony (Blushing Groom (FR))
025 unnamed 2 b c High Chaparral (IRE) - Pray (IRE) (Priolo (USA))

Lydia Pearce

Wroughton House Stables, 37 Old Station Road, Newmarket, Suffolk CB8 8DT

Tel: (Home) 01638 664669 **Fax:** 01638 669891 **MOBILE**: 07787 517864

OLDER HORSES

001 **BLACK ICEMAN** 5 bl g Iceman - Slite (Mind Games)
002 **COUNT CEPRANO** (IRE) 9 b g Desert Prince (IRE) - Camerlata (Common Grounds)
003 **DR FINLEY** (IRE) 6 ch g Dr Fong (USA) - Farrfesheena (USA) (Rahy (USA))
004 **DUKE OF ARICABEAU** (IRE) 4 ch g Modigliani (USA) - Essentialk Fear (IRE) (Pivotal)
005 **GHUFA** (IRE) 9 b g Sakhee (USA) - Hawriyah (USA) (Dayjur, USA))
006 **HATTA STREAM** (IRE) 7 b g Oasis Dream - Rubies From Burma (USA) (Forty Niner (USA))
007 **LAND HAWK** (IRE) 7 br g Trans Island - Heike (Glenstal (USA))
008 **MERCHANTS RETURN** 4 b g Byron - Molly Pitcher (IRE) (Halling (USA))
009 **NEWINGTON** 4 b f Iceman - Almunia (IRE) (Mujadil (USA))
010 **OLIMAMU** (IRE) 6 b m Barathea (IRE) - La Galeisa (IRE) (Warning)
011 **OLNEY LASS** 6 b m Lucky Story (USA) - Zalebe (Bahamian Bounty)
012 **PRINCESS PALMER** 4 b f Iceman - Tapas En Bal (FR) (Mille Balles (FR))

3 YEAR OLDS

013 **DAISIE CUTTER** 3 b f Tobougg (IRE) - Bowled Out (GER) (Dansili)
014 **SHAMALAD** 3 b c Shamardal (USA) - Steam Cuisine (Mark of Esteem (IRE))
015 **SWEET TALKING GUY** (IRE) 3 b g Oratorio (IRE) - Sweet Namibia (IRE) (Namid)

Tim Pitt

Frankland Lodge Stables, Hamilton Rd.,Newmarket CB8 7JQ
Correspondence to Hatchfield Farmhouse, Fordham Rd., Newmarket CB8 7XL

Tel: 01638 666344 **Mobile:** 07917 541341

OLDER HORSES

001 **DARK RANGER** 7 br g Where Or When (IRE) - Dark Raider (IRE) (Definite Article)
002 **MR RED CLUBS** (IRE) 4 b g Red Clubs (IRE) - Queen Cobra (IRE) (Indian Rocket)
003 **OUR JONATHAN** 6 b g Invincible Spirit (IRE) - Sheik'n Swing (Celtic Swing)

3 YEAR OLDS

004 **CHEROKEE PRINCESS** (IRE) 3 ch f Iffraaj - Radiancy (IRE) (Mujtahid (USA))
005 **DARK JUSTICE** (IRE) 3 b f Lawman (FR) - Dark Raider (IRE) (Definite Article)
006 **KATIE GALE** 3 b f Shirocco (GER) - Karla June (Unfuwain (USA))
007 **LAVENDER BAY** 3 b f Needwood Blade - In Good Faith (USA) (Dynaformer (USA))
008 **LIVELY LITTLE LADY** 3 b f Beat All (USA) - Ever So Lonely (Headin' Up)
009 **PEARL SPICE** (IRE) 3 ch g Dalakhani (IRE) - Cinnamon Rose (USA) (Trempolino (USA))
010 **SIOUX CHIEFTAIN** (IRE) 3 b g Mount Nelson - Lady Gin (USA) (Saint Ballado (CAN))

2 YEAR OLDS

011 **DARK TSARINA** (IRE) 2 b f Soviet Star (USA) - Dark Raider (IRE) (Definite Article)
012 **ONE CHANCE** (IRE) 2 b f Invincible Spirit (IRE) - Towards (USA) (Fusaichi Pegasus (USA))
013 **VALUED OPINION** (IRE) 2 b c Art Connoisseur (IRE) - Paix Royale (Royal Academy (USA))

Sir Mark Prescott, Bt.

Heath House, Moulton Road, Newmarket, Suffolk CB8 8DU

Tel: 01638 662117 **Fax:** 01638 666572

OLDER HORSES

001 **ALBAMARA** 4 b br f Galileo (IRE) - Albanova (Alzao (USA))
002 **ATHENIAN** (IRE) 4 b f Acclamation - Ziria (IRE) (Danehill Dancer (IRE))
003 **BETWEEN US** 4 b f Galileo (IRE) - Confidante (USA) (Dayjur (USA))
004 **CELESTIAL RAY** 4 ch c Pivotal - Heavenly Ray (USA) (Rahy (USA))
005 **ITALIAN RIVIERA** 4 b g Galileo (IRE) - Miss Corniche (Hernando (FR))
006 **MUTUAL REGARD** (IRE) 4 b g Hernando (FR) - Hidden Charm (IRE) (Big Shuffle (USA))
007 **PALLASATOR** 4 b g Motivator - Ela Athena (Ezzoud (IRE))
008 **REPEATER** 4 b g Montjeu (IRE) - Time Over (Mark of Esteem (IRE))

3 YEAR OLDS

009 **ALCAEUS** 3 b c Hernando (FR) - Alvarita (Selkirk (USA))
010 **ALWILDA** 3 gr f Hernando (FR) - Albanova (Alzao (USA))
011 **ALZAVOLA** 3 gr f With Approval (CAN) - Alizadora (Zilzal (USA))
012 **BIG THUNDER** 3 gr g Dalakhani (IRE) - Charlotte O Fraise (IRE) (Beat Hollow)
013 **CURIOUS MIND** 3 b f Dansili - Intrigued (Darshaan)
014 **INHERITED** 3 b g Selkirk (USA) - Akdariya (IRE) (Shirley Heights)
015 **KHOTAN** 3 b c Hernando (FR) - Miss Katmandu (IRE) (Rainbow Quest (USA))
016 **LYRIC PIECE** 3 ch f Dutch Art - Humouresque (Pivotal)
017 **MAN FROM SEVILLE** 3 ch g Duke of Marmalade (IRE) - Basanti (USA) (Galileo (IRE))
018 **NORTH POLE** 3 b g Compton Place - Cool Question (Polar Falcon (USA))
019 **PIGEON POWER** 3 b f Byron - Making Waves (IRE) (Danehill (USA))
020 **PORTRAIT** 3 ch f Peintre Celebre (USA) - Annalina (USA) (Cozzene (USA))
021 **SAGESSE** 3 ch f Smart Strike (CAN) - Summer Night (Nashwan (USA))
022 **SAVANNA LA MAR** (USA) 3 ch f Curlin (USA) - Soft Morning (Pivotal)
023 **SCALA ROMANA** (IRE) 3 b f Holy Roman Emperor (IRE) - Sliding Scale (Sadler's Wells (USA))
024 **SECRET SONG** 3 b g Singspiel (IRE) - Confidante (USA) (Dayjur (USA))
025 **SLIP OF THE TONGUE** 3 ch g Zamindar (USA) - Kiswahili (Selkirk (USA))
026 **SZABO'S ART** 3 br f Excellent Art - Violette (Observatory (USA))

2 YEAR OLDS

027 **BEWITCHMENT** 2 b f Pivotal - Hypnotize (Machiavellian (USA))
028 **CANNES MOUGINS** 2 b c Galileo (IRE) - Miss Riviera Golf (Hernando (FR))
029 **CHARLOTTE'S DAY** 2 b f Dalakhani (IRE) - Charlotte O Fraise (IRE) (Beat Hollow)
030 **CHINESE JADE** 2 gr c Cape Cross (IRE) - Chinese White (IRE) (Dalakhani (IRE))
031 **CLARICE** 2 b f Cape Cross (IRE) - Phillipina (Medicean)
032 **FLORA MEDICI** 2 b f Sir Percy - Florentia (Medicean)
033 **HOT REPLY** 2 br f Notnowcato - Cool Question (Polar Falcon (USA))
034 **MISS VERDOYANTE** 2 b f Montjeu (IRE) - Miss Provence (Hernando (FR))
035 MOUNTAIN KINGDOM (IRE) 2 b c Montjeu (IRE) - Althea Rose (IRE) (Green Desert (USA))
036 **NAMELY** (IRE) 2 b f Rock of Gibraltar (IRE) - Viz (IRE) (Darshaan)
037 **PALACE DRAGON** (IRE) 2 b c Lawman (FR) - Mayonga (IRE) (Dr Fong (USA))
038 **ROHESIA** 2 b f High Chaparral (IRE) - Common Knowledge (Rainbow Quest (USA))
039 **SANCUS** 2 ch g Compton Place - Blue Echo (Kyllachy)
040 **SARPECH** (IRE) 2 b c Sea The Stars (IRE) - Sadima (IRE) (Sadler's Wells (USA))
041 **SECRET KEEPER** 2 ch f New Approach (IRE) - Confidante (USA) (Dayjur (USA))
042 **SOIREE D'ETE** 2 b f Selkirk (USA) - Souvenance (Hernando (FR))
043 **SUNSET SHORE** 2 b f Oasis Dream - Summer Night (Nashwan (USA))
044 **THREETIMESALADY** 2 b f Royal Applause - Triple Joy (Most Welcome)
045 **UPSHOT** 2 b f Pivotal - Soar (Danzero (AUS))

Noel Quinlan

Harraton Stables, Chapel Street, Exning, Newmarket, Suffolk CB8 7HA

Tel: 01638 660464 (h) **Fax:** 01638 663282 **Mobile:** 07815 072946

OLDER HORSES

001 **BAHRAIN STORM** (IRE) 10 b g Bahhare (USA) - Dance Up A Storm (USA) (Storm Bird (CAN))
002 **BENEFIT EVENING** (IRE) 8 b g Beneficial - She Is Promising (IRE) (Henbit (USA))
003 **BURNS NIGHT** 7 ch g Selkirk (USA) - Night Frolic (Night Shift (USA))
004 **CHISWICK BEY** (IRE) 5 b g Elusive City (USA) - Victoria Lodge (IRE) (Grand Lodge (USA))
005 **FIRE IN BABYLON** (IRE) 5 b g Montjeu (IRE) - Three Owls (IRE) (Warning)
006 **JUDICIOUS** 6 ch g Pivotal - Virtuous (Exit To Nowhere (USA))
007 **KHAWATIM** 5 b g Intikhab (USA) - Don't Tell Mum (IRE) (Dansili)
008 **MOYNE NINEOSEVEN** (IRE) 7 b g Milan - Laprida (IRE) (Executive Perk)
009 **NELSON'S BAY** 4 b g Needwood Blade - In Good Faith (USA) (Dynaformer (USA))
010 **ORATORY** (IRE) 7 b g Danehill Dancer (IRE) - Gentle Night (Zafonic (USA))
011 **RUDIGREEN** (IRE) 10 b g Rudimentary (USA) - Green Avenue (IRE) (Satco (FR))
012 **SKY KHAN** 4 b g Cape Cross (IRE) - Starlit Sky (Galileo (IRE))
013 **TWEEDLE DEE** 4 b f Araafa (IRE) - Sismique (Warning)

3 YEAR OLDS

014 **BLAZEOFENCHANTMENT** (USA) 3 b c Officer (USA) - Willow Rush (USA) (Wild Rush (USA))
015 **DIXIE SKY** (USA) 3 b br f Dixie Union (USA) - Mona Quita (USA) (El Corredor (USA))
016 **EXCLUSION** (USA) 3 b br f Include (USA) - Long Silence (USA) (Alleged (USA))
017 **LOUCAL** 3 b c Lucky Story (USA) - Penny Ha'penny (Bishop of Cashel)
018 **MYSTERIOUS WONDER** 3 b g Oasis Dream - Raskutani (Dansili)
019 **SEVEN OF CLUBS** (IRE) 3 b c Red Clubs (IRE) - Solo Symphony (IRE) (Fayruz)
020 **VITRUVIAN LADY** 3 b f Manduro (GER) - Vas Y Carla (USA) (Gone West (USA))

2 YEAR OLDS

021 **ELSIE PARTRIDGE** (IRE) 2 b f Kodiac - La Bataille (USA) (Out of Place (USA))
022 **GENAX** (IRE) 2 b f Green Desert (USA) - Steam Cuisine (Mark of Esteem (IRE))
023 **GOLDEN SPEAR** 2 ch c Kyllachy - Penmayne (Inchinor)
024 **GRANDAD CHUNK** (IRE) 2 gr ro c Acclamation - Silverdreammachine (IRE) (Marju (IRE))
025 **LOVE IN THE DESERT** 2 b f Lemon Drop Kid (USA) - Jenny Lake (USA) (Danzig (USA))
026 **NONAGON** 2 b c Pastoral Pursuits - Nine Red (Royal Applause)
027 **SPEEDFIEND** 2 b c Bahamian Bounty - Vive Les Rouges (Acclamation)
028 **SWEET ACCLAIM** (IRE) 2 b f Acclamation - Wildsplash (USA) (Deputy Minister (CAN))
029 **THE DOYLE MACHINE** (IRE) 2 b g Camacho - Berenica (IRE) (College Chapel)
030 **WEISSE GIRL** 2 b f Halling (USA) - White Turf (GER) (Tiger Hill (IRE))

Mick Quinn

Southgate Barn (Southgate Stables), Hamilton Road, Newmarket CB8 0WY

Mobile: 07973 260054

NO HORSE LIST AVAILABLE AT TIME OF GOING TO PRESS

Mark Rimmer

Red House Stables, (2nd yard) Hamilton Road, Newmarket CB8 0TE
Correspondence to 2 Pine Tree Bungalows, Philips Close CB8 0PB

Tel: 01638 608540 (o) 01638 577498 (h) **Mobile:** 07913 111205

OLDER HORSES

001 **CORN MAIDEN** 4 b f Refuse To Bend (IRE) - Namat (IRE) (Daylami (IRE))

3 YEAR OLDS

002 **ANNALEY MY DARLING** (IRE) 3 b f Shamardal (USA) - Unreal (Dansili)
003 **GRAPES HILL** 3 b f Kingsalsa (USA) - Red Blossom (Green Desert (USA))

2 YEAR OLDS

004 **ECLIPTIC SUNRISE** 2 b f Compton Place - Winter Moon (Mujadil (USA))

John Ryan

Cadland Stables, Moulton Rd., Newmarket CB8 8DU

Tel: 01638 664172 **Tel:** (Home) 01638 731084 **Fax:** 01638 664172 **Mobile:** 07739 801235

OLDER HORSES

001 **FOCAIL MAITH** 5 b g Oratorio (IRE) – Glittering Image (Ire) (Sadler's Wells, USA))
002 **IF WHAT AND MAY BE** 5 ch g Needwood Blade – Pink Champagne (Cosmonaut)
003 **MASTERS BLAZING** 4 ch g Iceman – Loquacity (Diktat)
004 **OCEAN'S MINSTREL** 7 b g Pivotal – Minstrel's Dance (CAN) (Pleasant Colony, USA))
005 **OCEAN TEMPEST** 4 gr g Act One – Ipsa Loquitur (Unfuwain (USA))
006 **SOMEMOTHERSDOHAVEM** 4 ch g Avonbridge – Show Off (Efisio)
007 **SPIN AGAIN** (IRE) 8 b g Intikhab (USA) – Queen Of The May (IRE) (Nicolotte)
008 **THECORNISHCOCKNEY** 4 bl g Cockney Rebel (IRE) – Glittering Image (IRE) (Sadler's Wells, USA))
009 **THECORNISHCOWBOY** 4 b g Haafhd – Oriental Dance (Fantastic Light, USA))
010 **THECORNISHWREN** (IRE) 4 ch f Medecis – Coulisse (IRE) (In The Wings)
011 **WILDOMAR** 4 b g Kyllachy – Murrieta (Docksider, USA))

3-YEAR-OLDS

012 **OCEAN APPLAUSE** 3 b c Royal Applause – Aldora (Magic Ring (IRE)))
013 **ROYAL CAPER** 3 b g Royal Applause – Ukraine (IRE) (Cape Cross, IRE))

2-YEAR-OLDS

014 **APPLEJACK LAD** 2 ch c Three Valleys (USA) – Fittonia (FR) (Ashkalani, IRE)
015 **EVACUSAFE LADY** 2 ch f Avonbridge – Snow Shoes (Sri Pekan, USA))
016 Unnamed 2 f Rock Of Gibraltar (Ire) – Balliasta (IRE) (Grand Lodge, USA)
017 Unnamed 2 f Haatef (USA) – Common Charisma (IRE) (Highest Honor, FR))
018 Unnamed 2 c Nayef (USA) – Plucky (Kyllachy)

Dr Jon D Scargill

Red House Stables, Hamilton Road, Newmarket, Suffolk CB8 0TE

Tel: 01638 663254 **Fax:** 01638 667767

OLDER HORSES

001 **ASIA MINOR** (IRE) 4 ch f Pivotal - Anka Britannia (USA) (Irish River (FR))
002 **JUNKET** 6 b m Medicean - Gallivant (Danehill (USA))

3 YEAR OLDS

003 **MAN IN THE ARENA** 3 b g Bertolini (USA) - Torver (Lake Coniston (IRE))
004 **THE GINGER BERRY** 3 ch g First Trump - Dolly Coughdrop (IRE) (Titus Livius (FR))

David Simcock

Trillium Place Stables, Birdcage Walk, Newmarket, Suffolk CB8 0NE

Tel: 01638 662968 **Fax:** 01638 663888 **Mobile:** 07808 954109

OLDER HORSES

001 **AQUILLA** (IRE) 4 b f Teofilo (IRE) - Dance Troupe (Rainbow Quest (USA))
002 **ATTRACTION TICKET** 4 b g Selkirk (USA) - Trick (IRE) (Shirley Heights)
003 **BALDUCCI** 6 b g Dansili - Miss Meltemi (IRE) (Miswaki Tern (USA))
004 **CASPAR NETSCHER** 4 b c Dutch Art - Bella Cantata (Singspiel (IRE))
005 **CASTILO DEL DIABLO** (IRE) 4 br g Teofilo (IRE) - Hundred Year Flood (USA) (Giant's Causeway (USA))
006 **ENGLISH SUMMER** 6 b g Montjeu (IRE) - Hunt The Sun (Rainbow Quest (USA))
007 **GABRIAL'S GIFT** (IRE) 4 gr g Verglas (IRE) - Sahara Lady (IRE) (Lomitas)
008 **GABRIAL'S KING** (IRE) 4 b g Hurricane Run (IRE) - Danella (IRE) (Platini (GER))
009 **GRAMERCY** (IRE) 6 b g Whipper (USA) - Topiary (IRE) (Selkirk (USA))
010 **HAYLAMAN** (IRE) 5 b g Diamond Green (FR) - Schonbein (IRE) (Persian Heights)
011 **MABAIT** 7 b g Kyllachy - Czarna Roza (Polish Precedent (USA))
012 **MARTIN CHUZZLEWIT** (IRE) 4 ch g Galileo (IRE) - Alta Anna (FR) (Anabaa (USA))
013 **MOMENT IN TIME** (IRE) 4 b f Tiger Hill (IRE) - Horatia (IRE) (Machiavellian (USA))
014 **MONTASER** (IRE) 4 b g Rail Link - For Example (USA) (Northern Baby (CAN))
015 **NAVE** (USA) 6 b g Pulpit (USA) - Lakabi (USA) (Nureyev (USA))
016 **NO HERETIC** 5 b g Galileo (IRE) - Intrigued (Darshaan)
017 **NOBLE CITIZEN** (USA) 8 b g Proud Citizen (USA) - Serene Nobility (USA) (His Majesty (USA))
018 **OTTOMAN EMPIRE** (FR) 7 ch g Pivotal - Chesnut Bird (IRE) (Storm Bird (CAN))
019 **PRINCESS CAETANI** (IRE) 4 b f Dylan Thomas (IRE) - Caladira (IRE) (Darshaan)
020 **RED DUKE** (USA) 4 ch g Hard Spun (USA) - Saudia (USA) (Gone West (USA))
021 **SHEIKHZAYEDROAD** 4 b g Dubawi (IRE) - Royal Secrets (IRE) (Highest Honor (FR))
022 **TRADE STORM** 5 b h Trade Fair - Frisson (Slip Anchor)
023 **WAVEGUIDE** (IRE) 4 b f Dubawi (IRE) - Million Waves (IRE) (Mull of Kintyre (USA))
024 **WHISPERING WARRIOR** (IRE) 4 b c Oasis Dream - Varenka (IRE) (Fasliyev (USA))
025 **WHITE NILE** (IRE) 4 b c Galileo (IRE) - Super Gift (IRE) (Darshaan)

3 YEAR OLDS

026 **ARTY CAMPBELL** (IRE) 3 b g Dylan Thomas (IRE) - Kincob (USA) (Kingmaqmbo (USA))
027 **BIRDMAN** (IRE) 3 b g Danehill Dancer (IRE) - Gilded Vanity (IRE) (Indian Ridge)
028 **BRAZEN** 3 b c Kyllachy - Molly Brown (Rudimentary (USA))
029 **BRETON ROCK** (IRE) 3 b g Bahamian Bounty - Anna's Rock (IRE) (Rock Of Gibraltar (IRE))
030 **BRIGH** (IRE) 3 ch f Galileo (IRE) - La Vida Loca (IRE) (Caerleon (USA))
031 **CAFE SOCIETY** (FR) 3 b c Motivator - Mishina (FR) (Highest Honor (FR))
032 **COULD BE** (IRE) 3 b c Sakhee (USA) - Catch Us (FR) (Selkirk (USA))
033 **DEIRA PHANTOM** (IRE) 3 b c Cape Cross (IRE) - Ammo (IRE) (Sadler's Wells (USA))
034 **DREAM CAST** (IRE) 3 b c Refuse To Bend (IRE) - Star Studded (Cadeaux Genereux)
035 **EVERLASTING DREAM** 3 b f Oasis Dream - Magdalene (Act One)
036 **GABRIAL THE BOSS** (USA) 3 ch g Street Boss (USA) - Bacinella (USA) (El Gran Senor (USA))
037 **GABRIAL THE DUKE** (IRE) 3 ch g Duke of Marmalade (IRE) - Literacy (USA) (Diesis)
038 **GLASS OFFICE** 3 br gr c Verglas (IRE) - Oval Office (Pursuit of Love)
039 **GO ANGELLICA** (IRE) 3 ch f Kheleyf (USA) - Areyaam (USA) (Elusive Quality (USA))
040 **HERFUL SCHNERFUL** 3 b f Jeremy (USA) - Valandraud (IRE) (College Chapel)
041 **MAJEED** 3 b c Mount Nelson - Clever Millie (USA) (Cape Canaveral (USA))
042 **MARJU'S QUEST** (IRE) 3 b g Marju (IRE) - Queen's Quest (Rainbow Quest (USA))
043 **MIDNIGHT FLOWER** (IRE) 3 b f Haafhd - Takawiri (IRE) (Danehill (USA))
044 **MISS YOU TOO** 3 b f Montjeu (IRE) - Portrait of A Lady (IRE) (Peintre Celebre (USA))
045 **NEAMOUR** 3 b f Oasis Dream - Ever Rigg (Dubai Destination (USA))
046 **POSTE RESTANTE** 3 b f Halling (USA) - Postage Stampe (Singspiel (IRE))
047 **RAY WARD** (IRE) 3 b g Galileo (IRE) - Kentucky Warbler (IRE) (Spinning World (USA))

048 **SILK TRAIN** 3 b f Rail Link - Monsoon Wedding (Monsun (GER))
049 **WATERLILLY** (IRE) 3 b f Galileo (IRE) - Secret Garden (IRE) (Danehill (USA))
050 **WHISPERING** LADY (IRE) 3 b f Pivotal - Bon Nuit (IRE) (Night Shift (USA))
051 **ZEVA** 3 b f Zamindar (USA) - Mennetou (IRE) (Entrepreneur)

2 YEAR OLDS

052 **AFFAIRE DE COEUR** 2 b f Dalakhani (IRE) - Divergence (USA) (Red Ransom (USA))
053 **AL SHOOGH** 2 b f Nayef (USA) - Bakhoor (IRE) (Royal Applause)
054 **ALPS** 2 b f Danehill Dancer (IRE) - Mountain Chain (USA) (Royal Academy (USA))
055 **ANYA'S ANGEL** 2 b f Holy Roman Emperor (IRE) - Someone's Angel (USA) (Runaway Groom (CAN))
056 **BARYE** 2 b c Archipenko (USA) - Oblige (Robellino (USA))
057 **BORISOCRACY** (IRE) 2 b c Acclamation - River Mountain (Reset (AUS))
058 **BREUGHEL** (GER) 2 b c Dutch Art - Bezzaaf (Machiavellian (USA))
059 **CAN'T CHANGE IT** (IRE) 2 gr c Verglas (IRE) - All Tied Up (IRE) (Desert Prince (IRE))
060 **CLASSIFIED WEAPON** (USA) 2 b c Exchange Rate (USA) - Perfect Paula (USA) (Songandaprayer (USA))
061 **CURBYOURENTHUSIASM** 2 ch c Mastercraftsman (IRE) - Mohican Princess (Shirley Heights)
062 **DIEGO VELAZQUEZ** (IRE) 2 b c Duke of Marmalade (IRE) - Blessing (USA) (Pulpit (USA))
063 **DOCTOR SARDONICUS** 2 ch c Medicean - Never A Doubt (Night Shift (USA))
064 **ELLALAN** 2 b c Bahamian Bounty - Frabjous (Pivotal)
065 **ERRONEOUS** (IRE) 2 br c Footstepsinthesand - Atir Love (USA) (Green Dancer (USA))
066 **EYES FOR GOLD** (IRE) 2 ch c Galileo (IRE) - Baraka (IRE) (Danehill (USA))
067 **GREAT WAVE** (IRE) 2 b f Duke of Marmalade (IRE) - Rosamixa (FR) (Linamix (FR))
068 **HI LA MAL** 2 b c New Approach (IRE) - Dance Lively (USA) (Kingmambo (USA))
069 **JOIE DE REVE** (IRE) 2 b f Footstepsinthesand - La Caprice (USA) (Housebuster (USA))
070 **LORD EMPIRE** (IRE) 2 b c Invincible Spirit (IRE) - Miss Ghena (USA) (Gone West (USA))
071 **MADAME CHIANG** 2 b f Archipenko (USA) - Robe Chinoise (Robellino (USA))
072 **MOMENTUS** (IRE) 2 b f Montjeu (IRE) - Race For The Stars (USA) (Fusaichi Pegasus (USA))
073 **MORE ADORA** (IRE) 2 br f Dylan Thomas (IRE) - Niner's Home (USA) (Forty Niner (USA))
074 **NO EASY DAY** 2 b c Kheleyf (USA) - Komena (Komaite (USA))
075 **PURPLE LANE** (IRE) 2 ch c Danehill Dancer (IRE) - Big Heart (Mr Greeley (USA))
076 **SARIYAH** 2 b f Shirocco (GER) - Sakhya (IRE) (Barathea (IRE))
077 **SULTANTY** 2 b f Shamardal (USA) - Caught On Camera (Red Ransom (USA))
078 **SWAN LAKES** (IRE) 2 gr f Dalakhani (IRE) - Rock Salt (Selkirk (USA))
079 **TOO FRISKY** (IRE) 2 b g Rock of Gibraltar (IRE) - Delisha (Salse (USA))
080 **ULTRAVIOLET** (IRE) 2 b f Tamayuz - Aphorism (Halling (USA))
081 **VIGOR** (IRE) 2 b c Iffraaj - Miss Gibraltar (Rock of Gibraltar (IRE))
082 **WHISPERING STAR** (USA) 2 b br f War Front (USA) - Eclisse (FR) (Ski Chief (USA))
083 unnamed 2 b f Kheleyf (USA) - Areyaam (USA) (Elusive Quality (USA))
084 unnamed 2 b c High Chaparral (IRE) - Clincher Club (Polish Patriot (USA))
085 unnamed 2 b f Shamardal (USA) - Divisa (GER) (Lomitas)
086 unnamed 2 b f High Chaparral (IRE) - English Ballet (IRE) (Danehill Dancer (IRE))
087 unnamed 2 b f Nayef (USA) - Horatia (IRE) (Machiavellian (USA))
088 unnamed 2 b c Thewayyouare (USA) - Luck Be A Lady (IRE) (Alhaarth (IRE))
089 unnamed 2 ch c Street Cry (IRE) - Modesty Blaise (USA) (A P Indy (USA))
090 unnamed 2 b c Halling (USA) - Preceder (Polish Precedent (USA))
091 unnamed 2 b f Royal Applause - Pretty Majestic (IRE) (Invincible Spirit (IRE))
092 unnamed 2 b f Giant's Causeway (USA) - Swan Nebula (USA) (Seeking The Gold (USA))
093 unnamed 2 b f Fastnet Rock (AUS) - Uriah (GER) (Acatenango (GER))
094 unnamed 2 b c Galileo (IRE) - Walklikeanegyptian (IRE) (Danehill (USA))

Michael Squance

Meddler Stud, Bury Road, Kentford, Newmarket CB8 7PS
Correspondence to 36 Golden Miller Close, Newmarket CB8 7RT

Mobile: 07532 372557 **Mobile:** 07961 724658 **Tel:** 01638 664706 (h)

OLDER HORSES

001 **DIPLOMATIC** (IRE) 8 b g Cape Cross (IRE) - Embassy (Cadeaux Genereux)
002 **LADY CRICKETER** 4 b f Compton Place - Hickleton Lady (IRE) (Kala Shikari)

3 YEAR OLDS

003 **HARROGATE FAIR** 3 b g Trade Fair - Starbeck (IRE) (Spectrum (IRE))
004 **IFFLEY FIELDS** 3 b g Indesatchel (IRE) - Happy Omen (Warning)
005 **SIMPLY DREAMING** 3 b f Pastoral Pursuits - Tilly's Dream (Arkadian Hero (USA))

Eugene Stanford

Lemberg Stables, Hamilton Road, Newmarket, Suffolk, CB8 7JQ

Mobile: 07761 223096 **TEL:** 01638 660142

NO HORSE LIST AVAILABLE AT TIME OF GOING TO PRESS

William Stone

The Meadow, Streetly End, West Wickham, Cambridgeshire CB1 6RP

Mobile: 07788 971094 **TEL:** 01223 894617 (h)01223 894617

OLDER HORSES

001 **LACONICOS** (IRE) 11 ch g Foxhound (USA) – Thermopylae (Tenby)
001 **IMJIN RIVER** (IRE) 6 b g Namid – Lady Nasrana (FR) (Al Nasr, FR)
001 **WARDEN BOND** 5 ch g Monsieur Bond (IRE) – Warden Rose (Compton Place)

3 YEAR OLDS

001 **CLOCK OPERA** (IRE) 3 b f Excellent Art – Moving Diamonds (Lomitas)
001 **DANCE WITH DRAGONS** (IRE) 3 b g Namid – Duck Over (Warning)
001 **THREE CHOIRS** (IRE) 3 br f Rock Of Gibraltar (IRE) – Three Owls (Ire) (Warning)

Sir Michael Stoute

Freemason Lodge, Bury Road, Newmarket, Suffolk CB8 7BY

Tel: 01638 663801 **Fax:** 01638 667276

OLDER HORSES

001 **COMMEND** 4 ch g Pivotal - Reputable (Medicean)
002 **DANK** 4 b f Dansili - Masskana (IRE) (Darshaan)
003 **DUKE OF FIRENZE** 4 ch c Pivotal - Nannina (Medicean)
004 **ENROL** 4 b f Pivotal - Constitute (USA) (Gone West (USA))
005 **ESTIMATE** (IRE) 4 b f Monsun (GER) - Ebaziya (IRE) (Darshaan)
006 **GOSPEL CHOIR** 4 ch c Galileo (IRE) - Chorist (Pivotal)
007 **LABARINTO** 5 b g Dansili - Tarocchi (USA) (Affirmed (USA))
008 **LADYSHIP** 4 b f Oasis Dream - Peeress (Pivotal)
009 **LUCANIN** 4 b g Galileo (IRE) - Teggiano (IRE) (Mujtahid (USA))
010 **MARIA'S CHOICE** (IRE) 4 b g Oratorio (IRE) - Amathusia (Selkirk (USA))
011 **MAWAQEET** (USA) 4 b g Dynaformer (USA) - Lady Ilsley (USA) (Trempolino (USA))
012 **MODERN TUTOR** 4 b c Selkirk (USA) - Magical Romance (IRE) (Barathea (IRE))
013 **MR MAYNARD** 4 ch c Notnowcato - Crystal Cavern (USA) (Be My Guest (USA))
014 **OPINION** (IRE) 4 b c Oasis Dream - Kiltubber (IRE) (Sadler's Wells (USA))
015 **RYE HOUSE** (IRE) 4 b c Dansili - Threefold (USA) (Gulch (USA))
016 **SIR JOHN HAWKWOOD** (IRE) 4 b g Sir Percy - Athene (IRE) (Rousillon (USA))
017 **TALES OF GRIMM** (USA) 4 b c Distorted Humor (USA) - Stupendous Miss (USA) (Dynaformer (USA))
018 **ULTRASONIC** (USA) 4 b f Mizzen Mast (USA) - Quickfire (Dubai Millennium)

3 YEAR OLDS

019 **ABSEIL** (USA) 3 b c First Defence (USA) - Intercontinental (Danehill (USA))
020 **ALTHAROOS** (IRE) 3 br g Sakhee (USA) - Thamara (USA) (Street Cry (IRE))
021 **ARAB SPRING** (IRE) 3 b c Monsun (GER) - Spring Symphony (IRE) (Darshaan)
022 **ASTONISHING** (IRE) 3 b f Galileo (IRE) - Amazing Krisken (USA) (Kris S (USA))
023 **ASTORGS GALAXY** 3 b f Galileo (IRE) - Astorg (USA) (Lear Fan (USA))
024 **AULD ALLIANCE** (IRE) 3 b f Montjeu (IRE) - Highland Gift (IRE) (Generous (IRE))
025 **AVIETTA** (IRE) 3 gr f Dalakhani (IRE) - Alabastrine (Green Desert (USA))
026 **BAIHAS** 3 b c Nayef (USA) - Allegretto (IRE) (Galileo (IRE))
027 **BEDOUIN INVADER** (IRE) 3 b g Oasis Dream - Hovering (IRE) (In The Wings)
028 **BEEP** 3 b f Beat Hollow - Dialing Tone (USA) (Distant View (USA))
029 **BERKELEY STREET** (USA) 3 b g Street Cry (IRE) - Dream Ticket (USA) (Danzig (USA))
030 **BOHEMIAN DANCE** (IRE) 3 br f Dansili - Islington (IRE) (Sadler's Wells (USA))
031 **BOLD SNIPER** 3 b c New Approach (IRE) - Daring Aim (Daylami (IRE))
032 **CALL AHEAD** 3 ch f Three Valleys (USA) - Payphone (Anabaa (USA))
033 **CENTRED** (IRE) 3 gr f Dalakhani (IRE) - Drama Class (IRE) (Caerleon (USA))
034 **CHENGHO** (USA) 3 b g Henrythenavigator (USA) - Christmas In Aiken (USA) (Affirmed (USA))
035 **CIRCUS TURN** (USA) 3 b g Street Cry (IRE) - Showlady (USA) (Theatrical)
036 **CLAIM** (IRE) 3 b g Acclamation - Raysiza (IRE) (Alzao (USA))
037 **COULD IT BE** (IRE) 3 b f Galileo (IRE) - Butterfly Cove (USA) (Storm Cat (USA))
038 **DAMBUSTER** (IRE) 3 b g Dalakhani (IRE) - Threefold (USA) (Gulch (USA))
039 **DEFENDANT** 3 b c Medicean - Razzle (USA) (Danzig (USA))
040 **DREAM WILD** 3 b f Oasis Dream - Wince (Selkirk (USA))
041 **DUKE COSIMO** 3 ch g Pivotal - Nannina (Medicean)
042 **ECONOMY** 3 gr c Dalakhani (IRE) - Quiff (Sadler's Wells (USA))
043 **ELIK** (IRE) 3 b f Dalakhani (IRE) - Elopa (GER) (Tiger Hill (IRE))
044 **ENOBLED** 3 b c Dansili - Peeress (Pivotal)
045 **EVANGELIST** 3 b c Oasis Dream - Hi Calypso (IRE) (In The Wings)
046 **FANTASY IN BLUE** 3 b f Galileo (IRE) - Blue Symphony (Darshaan)
047 **GLAMOUR AND STYLE** (USA) 3 b f Dynaformer (USA) - Sometime (IRE) (Royal Academy (USA))

048 **GOLDEN TOUCH** 3 b c Galileo (IRE) - Approach (Darshaan)
049 **HILLSTAR** 3 b c Danehill Dancer (IRE) - Crystal Star (Mark of Esteem (IRE))
050 **INTEGRAL** 3 b f Dalakhani (IRE) - Echelon (Danehill (USA))
051 **INTRINSIC** 3 b c Oasis Dream - Infallible (Pivotal)
052 **JAREEDA** (USA) 3 b br f First Samurai (USA) - Manaal (USA) (Bahri (USA))
053 **JUST DARCY** 3 b f Danehill Dancer (IRE) - Jane Austen (IRE) (Galileo (IRE))
054 **KING'S REQUEST** (IRE) 3 ch g New Approach (IRE) - Palace Weekend (USA) (Seattle Dancer (USA))
055 **LEGENDS** (IRE) 3 b c Medaglia d'Oro (USA) - Elusive Legend (USA) (Elusive Quality (USA))
056 **LIBER NAUTICUS** (IRE) 3 b f Azamour (IRE) - Serres (IRE) (Daylami (IRE))
057 **LOVE MAGIC** 3 b f Dansili - Magical Romance (IRE) (Barathea (IRE))
058 **MADAME VESTRIS** (IRE) 3 ch f Galileo (IRE) - Mrs Lindsay (USA) (Theatrical)
059 **MANGO DIVA** 3 b f Holy Roman Emperor (IRE) - Mango Mischief (IRE) (Desert King (IRE))
060 **MAYPOLE LASS** 3 ch f Halling (USA) - Maigold Lass (Mark of Esteem (IRE))
061 **MEDDLING** 3 ch f Halling (USA) - Piffling (Pivotal)
062 **MISSION APPROVED** 3 b c Dansili - Moon Search (Rainbow Quest (USA))
063 **MUTAJALLY** 3 b c Teofilo (IRE) - Dhelaal (Green Desert (USA))
064 **NORTHERN MEETING** (IRE) 3 b f Dylan Thomas (IRE) - Scottish Stage (IRE) (Selkirk (USA))
065 **OMNIPRESENT** 3 b c Rail Link - Protectress (Hector Protector (USA))
066 **OTROOHA** (IRE) 3 b f Oasis Dream - Mumayeza (Indian Ridge)
067 **PAVLOSK** (USA) 3 b f Arch (USA) - Tsar's Pride (Sadler's Wells (USA))
068 **PERSEPOLIS** (IRE) 3 gr c Dansili - La Persiana (Daylami (IRE))
069 **PLAYBILL** 3 b f Medicean - Set The Scene (IRE) (Sadler's Wells (USA))
070 **PLOVER** 3 b f Oasis Dream - Short Dance (USA) (Hennessy (USA))
071 **PRESSURE POINT** 3 b c Oasis Dream - Arrive (Kahyasi)
072 **PROXIMATE** 3 b g Nayef (USA) - Contiguous (USA) (Danzig (USA))
073 **QAREENAH** (USA) 3 b f Arch (USA) - Princess Kris (Kris)
074 **RAUSHAN** (IRE) 3 gr f Dalakhani (IRE) - Chiang Mai (IRE) (Sadler's Wells (USA))
075 **RUN WITH PRIDE** (IRE) 3 b g Invincible Spirit (IRE) - Zibilene (Rainbow Quest (USA))
076 **RUSSIAN REALM** 3 b c Dansili - Russian Rhythm (USA) (Kingmambo (USA))
077 **SHADES OF SILVER** 3 b g Dansili - Silver Pivotal (IRE) (Pivotal)
078 **STOMACHION** (IRE) 3 b c Duke of Marmalade (IRE) - Insight (FR) (Sadler's Wells (USA))
079 **STRENGTH AND HONOR** (IRE) 3 b c Galileo (IRE) - Kasora (IRE) (Darshaan)
080 **TAFAASEEL** (USA) 3 b f Mr Greeley (USA) - Wasseema (USA) (Danzig (USA))
081 **TELESCOPE** (IRE) 3 b c Galileo (IRE) - Velouette (Darshaan)
082 **THEODORE GERICAULT** (IRE) 3 b g Sir Percy - Tableau Vivant (IRE) (Pivotal)
083 **VITAL EVIDENCE** (USA) 3 b c Empire Maker (USA) - Promising Lead (Danehill (USA))
084 **WAILA** 3 ch f Notnowcato - Crystal Cavern (USA) (Be My Guest (USA))
085 **WEST OF THE MOON** 3 ch f Pivotal - Canda (USA) (Storm Cat (USA))

2 YEAR OLDS

086 **ADORE** 2 b f Oasis Dream - Fantasize (Groom Dancer (USA))
087 **ALEX VINO** (IRE) 2 b c High Chaparral (IRE) - Rare Ransom (Oasis Dream)
088 **ALMUHEET** 2 b c Dansili - Arwaah (IRE) (Dalakhani (IRE))
089 **ALONG AGAIN** (IRE) 2 b f Elusive City (USA) - American Adventure (USA) (Miswaki (USA))
090 **ALTAAYIL** (IRE) 2 br c Sea The Stars (IRE) - Alleluia (Caerleon (USA))
091 **ARBAAB** 2 br c Dynaformer (USA) - Kaseema (USA) (Storm Cat (USA))
092 **ASYAD** (IRE) 2 b f New Approach (IRE) - Elle Danzig (GER) (Roi Danzig (USA))
093 **BRAGGING** (USA) 2 b br f Exchange Rate (USA) - Boasting (USA) (Kris S (USA))
094 **CANNOCK CHASE** (USA) 2 b c Lemon Drop Kid (USA) - Lynnwood Chase (USA) (Horse Chestnut (SAF))
095 **DALMATIA** (IRE) 2 gr f Cape Cross (IRE) - Dalataya (IRE) (Sadler's Wells (USA))
096 **DIANORA** 2 b f New Approach (IRE) - Nannina (Medicean)
097 **EXECUTRIX** 2 b f Oasis Dream - Exclusive (Polar Falcon (USA))
098 **EXTENT** 2 ch f Exceed And Excel (AUS) - Selkirk Sky (Selkirk (USA))
099 **EYE CONTACT** 2 br c Dansili - Modern Look (Zamindar (USA))
100 **FESTIVAL THEATRE** (IRE) 2 ch c Danehill Dancer (IRE) - Scottish Stage (IRE) (Selkirk (USA))
101 **FITNAH** (IRE) 2 b f Sea The Stars (IRE) - Ecoutila (USA) (Rahy (USA))
102 **FREEMASON** 2 b c Cape Cross (IRE) - Candy Mountain (Selkirk (USA))
103 **GHAAWY** 2 b c Teofilo (IRE) - Asawer (IRE) (Darshaan)

104 **GOOD VALUE** 2 ch c Champs Elysees - Change Course (Sadler's Wells (USA))
105 **GOTHIC** 2 b c Danehill Dancer (IRE) - Riberac (Efisio)
106 **HEHO** 2 b f Dansili - Nitya (FR) (Indian Ridge)
107 **HIGH STAND** 2 b c Kyllachy - Maugwenna (Danehill (USA))
108 **IDEA** (USA) 2 gr c Mizzen Mast (USA) - Discuss (USA) (Danzig (USA))
109 **INHERITANCE** 2 b f Oasis Dream - Peeress (Pivotal)
110 **JONE DES CHAMPS** (IRE) 2 b c Montjeu (IRE) - Desert Bloom (IRE) (Pilsudski (IRE))
111 **JUVENILE LEAD** (IRE) 2 ch c Sea The Stars (IRE) - Drama Class (IRE) (Caerleon (USA))
112 **KINGS FETE** 2 b c King's Best (USA) - Village Fete (Singspiel (IRE))
113 **MAIRISE** 2 b c Authorized (IRE) - Maigold Lass (Mark of Esteem (IRE))
114 **MARDIE GRAS** 2 ch f Galileo (IRE) - Midnight Angel (GER) (Acatenango (GER))
115 **MEZEL** 2 b c Tamayuz - Mumayeza (Indian Ridge)
116 **MONTONE** (IRE) 2 ch c Danehill Dancer (IRE) - Leocorno (IRE) (Pivotal)
117 **MUNAASER** 2 b c New Approach (IRE) - Safwa (IRE) (Green Desert (USA))
118 **NOBLE DESCENT** 2 ch f Pivotal - Noble Lady (Primo Dominie)
119 **PAS DE CHEVAL** (IRE) 2 ch c Pivotal - Olympienne (IRE) (Sadler's Wells (USA))
120 **PIVOTAL BRIDE** 2 ch f Dubawi (IRE) - Brazilian Bride (IRE) (Pivotal)
121 **PSYCHOMETRY** (FR) 2 b f Danehill Dancer (IRE) - Seven Magicians (USA) (Silver Hawk (USA))
122 **QAFFAAL** (USA) 2 b c Street Cry (IRE) - Wasseema (USA) (Danzig (USA))
123 **QUEEN'S PRIZE** 2 b f Dansili - Daring Aim (Daylami (IRE))
124 **RADIATOR** 2 b f Dubawi (IRE) - Heat Haze (Green Desert (USA))
125 **RAMSHACKLE** 2 b f Dansili - Purissima (USA) (Fusaichi Pegasus (USA))
126 **ROCHAMBEAU** (IRE) 2 b c Sir Percy - Tableau Vivant (IRE) (Pivotal)
127 **ROCKET SHIP** 2 b c Sinndar (IRE) - Bimini (Sadler's Wells (USA))
128 **ROYAL SEAL** 2 b f Dansili - Queen's Best (King's Best (USA))
129 **SEA THE BLOOM** 2 b f Sea The Stars (IRE) - Red Bloom (Selkirk (USA))
130 **SHAMA'S SONG** (IRE) 2 b f Teofilo (IRE) - Green Dollar (IRE) (Kingmambo (USA))
131 **SIR ROSCO** 2 b c Sir Percy - Rosacara (Green Desert (USA))
132 **SNOW SKY** 2 b c Nayef (USA) - Winter Silence (Dansili)
133 **SONG OF NAMIBIA** (IRE) 2 br c Cape Cross (IRE) - Spring Symphony (IRE) (Darshaan)
134 **STAMPEDE** (IRE) 2 b c High Chaparral (IRE) - Summerhill Parkes (Zafonic (USA))
135 **SURCINGLE** (USA) 2 b f Empire Maker (USA) - Promising Lead (Danehill (USA))
136 **TALL SHIP** (IRE) 2 b c Sea The Stars (IRE) - Magical Romance (IRE) (Barathea (IRE))
137 **TAMASHA** 2 ch f Sea The Stars (IRE) - Tamarind (IRE) (Sadler's Wells (USA))
138 **TERCEL** (IRE) 2 b c Monsun (GER) - Kitty Hawk (Danehill Dancer (IRE))
139 **TIME SIGNAL** 2 b f Champs Elysees - Sandglass (Zafonic (USA))
140 **TOP TUG** (IRE) 2 ch c Halling (USA) - Top Romance (IRE) (Entrepreneur)
141 **UPPER STREET** (IRE) 2 b f Dansili - Islington (IRE) (Sadler's Wells (USA))
142 unnamed 2 b c Montjeu (IRE) - Festoso (IRE) (Diesis)
143 unnamed 2 gr c Oasis Dream - Shreyas (IRE) (Dalakhani (IRE))

James Tate

Jamesfield Place, Hamilton Road, NEWMARKET, Suffolk, CB8 7JQ

Tel: 01638 669861 **FAX:** 01638 676634 **Mobile:** 07703 601283

NO HORSE LIST AVAILABLE AT TIME OF GOING TO PRESS

James A R Toller

Eve Lodge Stables, Hamilton Road, Newmarket, Suffolk CB8 0NY

Tel: 01638 668918 **Fax:** 01638 669384 **Mobile:** 07887 942234

OLDER HORSES

001 **ALEZANNA** 4 ch f Halling (USA) - Denica (IRE) (Night Shift (USA))
002 **LOVING SPIRIT** 5 b g Azamour (IRE) - Lolla's Spirit (IRE) (Montjeu (IRE))
003 **REWARDED** 4 b g Motivator - Granted (FR) (Cadeaux Genereux)
004 **SOHAR** 5 b m Iceman - Desert Joy (Daylami (IRE))
005 **SOHO SUSIE** (IRE) 4 br f Montjeu (IRE) - Lucina (Machiavellian (USA))

3 YEAR OLDS

006 **CHANDELLE CELESTE** 3 ch f Septieme Ciel (USA) - First Candlelight (First Trump)
007 **CHERRY TIGER** 3 b c Tiger Hill (IRE) - Lolla's Spirit (IRE) (Montjeu (IRE))
008 **CHESTER ROW** 3 ch c Compton Place - Sophie's Girl (Bahamian Bounty)
009 **GIVE US A REASON** 3 b f Motivator - Ela's Giant (Giant's Causeway (USA))
010 **LIVING DESERT** 3 gr g Oasis Dream - Sell Out (Act One)
011 **RED PILGRIM** (IRE) 3 b c Authorized (IRE) - Plenty of Action (USA) (Hennessy (USA))
012 **SHORT SHRIFT** (IRE) 3 ch f Nayef (USA) - Dusty Answer (Zafonic (USA))
013 **SMOKETHATTHUNDERS** (IRE) 3 gr g Elusive City (USA) - Zinstar (IRE) (Sinndar (IRE))
014 **SOHO DANCER** 3 b f Galileo (IRE) - River Belle (Lahib (USA))
015 **SUNNY HOLLOW** 3 b f Beat Hollow - Corndavon (USA) (Sheikh Albadou)

2 YEAR OLDS

016 **GANGES** (IRE) 2 b c Shamardal (USA) - Quantum (IRE) (Alhaarth (IRE))
017 **MAJESTIC SONG** 2 b f Royal Applause - Sakhee's Song (IRE) (Sakhee (USA))
018 **REEDCUTTER** 2 b c Passing Glance - Violet's Walk (Dr Fong (USA))

Mark H Tompkins

Exeter Ride, The Watercourse, Newmarket, Suffolk CB8 8LW

Tel: 01638 661434 **Fax:** 01638 668107 **Mobile:** 07799 663339

OLDER HORSES

001 **AKULA** (IRE) 6 ch g Soviet Star (USA) - Danielli (IRE) (Danehill (USA))
002 **ASTROGOLD** 4 ch f Motivator - Mega (IRE) (Petardia)
003 **ASTROMAGICK** 5 b m Rainbow Quest (USA) - Astrocharm (IRE) (Charnwood Forest (IRE))
004 **ASTROSCARLET** 4 ch f Carnival Dancer - Astrolove (IRE) (Bigstone (IRE))
005 **BARWICK** 5 b g Beat Hollow - Tenpence (Bob Back (USA))
006 **CHANKILLO** 4 ch g Observatory (USA) - Seasonal Blossom (IRE) (Fairy King (USA))
007 **COMRADE BOND** 5 ch g Monsieur Bond (IRE) - Eurolink Cafe (Grand Lodge (USA))
008 **DAZINSKI** 7 ch g Sulamani (IRE) - Shuheb (Nashwan (USA))
009 **EANANS BAY** (IRE) 4 b g Tiger Hill (IRE) - Gold Hush (USA) (Seeking The Gold (USA))
010 **JOE THE COAT** 4 ch g Act One - Torcross (Vettori (IRE))
011 **LIKE CLOCKWORK** 4 b g Rail Link - Tenpence (Bob Back (USA))
012 **MY GUARDIAN ANGEL** 4 b g Araafa (IRE) - Angels Guard You (Bahamian Bounty)
013 **SMOKEY OAKEY** (IRE) 9 b g Tendulkar (USA) - Veronica (Persian Bold)
014 **STAR COMMANDER** 5 b g Desert Style (IRE) - Barakat (Bustino)
015 **TOPTEMPO** 4 ch f Halling (USA) - Topatoo (Bahamian Bounty)
016 **ZENARINDA** 6 b m Zamindar (USA) - Tenpence (Bob Back (USA))

3 YEAR OLDS

017 **ASTROSAPPHIRE** 3 b f Manduro (GER) - Astromancer (USA) (Silver Hawk (USA))
018 **BARBSIZ** (IRE) 3 ch f Elnadim (USA) - Bianca Cappello (IRE) (Glenstal (USA))
019 **FREDERICK ALFRED** 3 ch c Halling (USA) - Trew Class (Inchinor)
020 **LIKELIKELIKELIKEIT** 3 b f Avonbridge - Rutland Water (IRE) (Hawk Wing (USA))
021 **MARSH DRAGON** 3 b f Beat Hollow - Qilin (IRE) (Second Set (IRE))
022 **STAR OF MISSOURI** 3 ch g Namid - Missouri (Charnwood Forest (IRE))
023 **TOPAMICHI** 3 b g Beat Hollow - Topatori (IRE) (Topanoora)

2 YEAR OLDS

024 **ASTROCAT** 2 b f Zamindar (USA) - Mega (IRE) (Petardia)
025 **ASTRODIAMOND** 2 b f Black Sam Bellamy (IRE) - Astromancer (USA) (Silver Hawk (USA))
026 **ASTROWOLF** 2 b c Halling (USA) - Optimistic (Reprimand)
027 **BLUE BOUNTY** 2 ch c Bahamian Bounty - Laheen (IRE) (Bluebird (USA))
028 **CRYSTAL PEARL** 2 b f Beat Hollow - Missouri (Charnwood Forest (IRE))
029 **LITTLE TINKA** 2 b f Three Valleys (USA) - Tenpence (Bob Back (USA))
030 **MY LITTLE FRIEND** 2 ch c Pastoral Pursuits - Sosumi (Be My Chief (USA))
031 **NANCY** 2 b f Rail Link - Feabhas (IRE) (Spectrum (IRE))
032 **SEE ME SOMETIME** 2 ch c Observatory (USA) - Nice Time (IRE) (Tagula (IRE))
033 **SWILKEN** 2 ch c Halling (USA) - Azure Mist (Bahamian Bounty)
034 **TOPALING** 2 ch f Halling (USA) - Topatori (IRE) (Topanoora)
035 **TRAIN SET** 2 b c Sakhee (USA) - Dolls House (Dancing Spree (USA))

Roger Varian

Kremlin House Stables, Fordham Road, NEWMARKET, Suffolk, CB8 7AQ

Tel: 01638 661702 **Fax:** 01638 667018 **Mobile:** 07879 414664

OLDER HORSES

001 **ALJAMAAHEER** (IRE) 4 ch c Dubawi (IRE) - Kelly Nicole (IRE) (Rainbow Quest (USA))
002 **AMBIVALENT** (IRE) 4 b f Authorized (IRE) - Darrery (Darshaan)
003 **CAMERON HIGHLAND** (IRE) 4 b c Galileo (IRE) - Landmark (USA) (Arch (USA))
004 **DANCEWITHTHEDEVIL** (SAF) 7 b m Modus Vivendi - Emperor's Dance (SAF) (Caesour (USA))
005 **EKTIHAAM** (IRE) 4 b g Invincible Spirit (IRE) - Liscune (IRE) (King's Best (USA))
006 **ETON FOREVER** (IRE) 6 b g Oratorio (IRE) - True Joy (IRE) (Zilzal (USA))
007 **FARRAAJ** (IRE) 4 b g Dubai Destination (USA) - Pastorale (Nureyev (USA))
008 **FRASERS HILL** 4 ch c Selkirk (USA) - Shemriyna (IRE) (King of Kings (IRE))
009 **JUSTINEO** 4 b c Oasis Dream - Loulwa (IRE) (Montjeu (IRE))
010 **MIJHAAR** 5 b g Shirocco (GER) - Jathaabeh (Nashwan (USA))
011 **OOJOOBA** 4 b f Monsun (GER) - Ameerat (Mark of Esteem (IRE))
012 **PANETTONE** (IRE) 4 b f Montjeu (IRE) - Tea Break (Daylami (IRE))
013 **SOUND HEARTS** (USA) 4 b br f Sir Percy - Crystal Seas (Zamindar (USA))
014 **SRI PUTRA** 7 b h Oasis Dream - Wendylina (IRE) (In The Wings)
015 **STEPS** (IRE) 5 br g Verglas (IRE) - Killinallan (Vettori (IRE))
016 **TAFAWUK** (USA) 4 b g Nayef (USA) - Yaqeen (Green Desert (USA))
017 **ZANOTTI** 4 b g Authorized (IRE) - Majestic Sakeena (IRE) (King's Best (USA))

3 YEAR OLDS

018 **AGERZAM** 3 b c Holy Roman Emperor (IRE) - Epiphany (Zafonic (USA))
019 **AGLAOPHONOS** 3 ch g Dutch Art - Lasting Image (Zilzal (USA))
020 **ALOHA** 3 b f With Approval (CAN) - Almamia (Hernando (FR))
021 **ARDINGLY** (IRE) 3 b f Danehill Dancer (IRE) - Asnieres (USA) (Spend A Buck (USA))
022 **ASHAADD** (IRE) 3 b g Dansili - Vital Statistics (Indian Ridge)
023 **AZENZAR** 3 b f Danehill Dancer (IRE) - Dashing (IRE) (Sadler's Wells (USA))
024 **BASTION** (USA) 3 b c Giant's Causeway (USA) - Marital Spook (USA) (Silver Ghost (USA))
025 **BIG FORTUNE** 3 b c Motivator - Small Fortune (Anabaa (USA))
026 **CAUBERG** 3 b c Green Desert (USA) - Thorntoun Piccolo (Groom Dancer (USA))
027 **CHELWOOD GATE** (IRE) 3 b gr c Aussie Rules (USA) - Jusoor (USA) (El Prado (IRE))
028 **CHITTENDEN** (USA) 3 b f Raven's Pass (USA) - Port Roberto (USA) (Dynaformer (USA))
029 **DEGLET NOOR** 3 br f New Approach (IRE) - Almoutezah (USA) (Storm Cat (USA))
030 **DUCAB** (IRE) 3 b g Dansili - Twyla Tharp (IRE) (Sadler's Wells (USA))
031 **DUROBLE MAN** 3 b g Manduro (GER) - Jalousie (IRE) (Barathea (IRE))
032 **ELKAAYED** (USA) 3 ch c Distorted Humor (USA) - Habibti (USA) (Tabasco Cat (USA))
033 **ELSINIAAR** 3 bl c New Approach (IRE) - Comic (IRE) (Be My Chief (USA))
034 **ERSAAL** 3 b g Dubawi (IRE) - Makaaseb (USA) (Pulpit (USA))
035 **EXCEPTIONELLE** 3 br f Exceed And Excel (AUS) - Turning Leaf (IRE) (Last Tycoon)
036 **FAMILLIARITY** 3 ch f Nayef (USA) - Millistar (Galileo (IRE))
037 **HASHEEM** 3 ch c New Approach (IRE) - Masaafat (Act One)
038 **HAZZAAT** (IRE) 3 ch g Iffraaj - Hurricane Irene (IRE) (Green Desert (USA))
039 **HEKAAYAAT** (USA) 3 ch f Mr Greeley (USA) - Mostaqeleh (USA) (Rahy (USA))
040 **HORSTED KEYNES** (FR) 3 ch c Giant's Causeway (USA) - Viking's Cove (USA) (Miswaki (USA))
041 **HUFFOOF** (IRE) 3 b f Dalakhani (IRE) - Albahja (Sinndar (IRE))
042 **IFFRAAJ PINK** (IRE) 3 b f Iffraaj - Red Vale (IRE) (Halling (USA))
043 **JALADEE** 3 b c Cape Cross (IRE) - Atamana (IRE) (Lahib (USA))
044 **KABBAAS** (IRE) 3 ch g Pivotal - Dorrati (USA) (Dubai Millennium)
045 **KOHLAAN** (IRE) 3 b g Elusive City (USA) - Rock Salt (Selkirk (USA))
046 **LANANSAAK** (IRE) 3 ch f Zamindar (USA) - Bunood (IRE) (Sadler's Wells (USA))
047 **MIGUEL GRAU** (USA) 3 b g City Zip (USA) - Zuri Ridge (USA) (Cox's Ridge (USA))

048 **MORAWIJ** 3 ch c Exceed And Excel (AUS) - Sister Moonshine (FR) (Piccolo)
049 **MUTASHADED** (USA) 3 b c Raven's Pass (USA) - Sortita (GER) (Monsun (GER))
050 **MUTHMERA** (USA) 3 b f Dynaformer (USA) - Burooz (IRE) (King's Best (USA))
051 **MYLINGTON** LIGHT 3 ch f Mount Nelson - Atlantic Light (Linamix (FR))
052 **NAALATT** (IRE) 3 b f Dansili - Vine Street (IRE) (Singspiel (IRE))
053 **ONE PEKAN** (IRE) 3 b c Hard Spun (USA) - Stormy Blessing (USA) (Storm Cat (USA))
054 **ORBISON** (IRE) 3 b g Azamour (IRE) - Glenmara (USA) (Known Fact (USA))
055 **PRINCESS LOULOU** (IRE) 3 ch f Pivotal - Aiming (Highest Honor (FR))
056 **PYREXIA** 3 br g Singspiel (IRE) - Street Fire (IRE) (Street Cry (IRE))
057 **QAWAAFY** (USA) 3 b f Street Cry (IRE) - Eswarah (Unfuwain (USA))
058 **RAVEN'S ROCK** (IRE) 3 b g Raven's Pass (USA) - Delphinus (Soviet Star (USA))
059 **RIBAAT** (IRE) 3 b c Invincible Spirit (IRE) - Fonda (USA) (Quiet American (USA))
060 **ROCKY GROUND** (IRE) 3 b c Acclamation - Keriyka (IRE) (Indian Ridge)
061 **SAADATT** 3 b f New Approach (IRE) - Ameerat (Mark of Esteem (IRE))
062 **SEVERIANO** (USA) 3 b g Danehill Dancer (IRE) - Time Control (Sadler's Wells (USA))
063 **SHEMAAL** (IRE) 3 b c Monsun (GER) - Zahrat Dubai (Unfuwain (USA))
064 **SINISTER** (IRE) 3 b c Sinndar (IRE) - Shamsada (IRE) (Kahyasi)
065 **SOARING SPIRITS** (IRE) 3 ch g Tamayuz - Follow My Lead (Night Shift (USA))
066 **STAR PEARL** (USA) 3 b f Tapit (USA) - Lexi Star (USA) (Crypto Star (USA))
067 **TAJHEEZ** (IRE) 3 b g Raven's Pass (USA) - Ghaidaa (IRE) (Cape Cross (IRE))
068 **TANTSHI** (IRE) 3 b f Invincible Spirit (IRE) - Qasirah (IRE) (Machiavellian (USA))
069 **TENOR** (IRE) 3 b c Oratorio (IRE) - Cedar Sea (IRE) (Persian Bold)
070 **TUSCAN FUN** 3 ch g Medicean - Elfin Laughter (Alzao (USA))
071 **TWARY** (USA) 3 b g Indian Charlie (USA) - Street Sounds (CAN) (Street Cry (IRE))
072 **WILHANA** (IRE) 3 b f Singspiel (IRE) - Jathaabeh (Nashwan (USA))
073 **YARROOM** (IRE) 3 b c Cape Cross (IRE) - Aryaamm (IRE) (Galileo (IRE))
074 **YOU LOOK SO GOOD** 3 gr f Excellent Art - Divine Grace (IRE) (Definite Article)
075 unnamed 3 b br g Authorized (IRE) - Henties Bay (IRE) (Cape Cross (IRE))

2 YEAR OLDS

076 **ALJAAZIAH** 2 b br f Medaglia d'Oro (USA) - Eswarah (Unfuwain (USA))
077 **ALMASHOOQA** (USA) 2 b br f Dubawi (IRE) - Almoutezah (USA) (Storm Cat (USA))
078 **ANDHESONTHERUN** (IRE) 2 b c Captain Rio - Harvest Joy (IRE) (Daggers Drawn (USA))
079 **AYRAD** (IRE) 2 ch c Dalakhani (IRE) - Sweet Firebird (IRE) (Sadler's Wells (USA))
080 **BAAREZ** (USA) 2 ch c Hard Spun (USA) - Sortita (GER) (Monsun (GER))
081 **CLASSICAL ART** (IRE) 2 ch c Excellent Art - Ask Carol (IRE) (Foxhound (USA))
082 **DORRAAR** (IRE) 2 b f Shamardal (USA) - Dorrati (USA) (Dubai Millennium)
083 **DOUBLE UP** 2 b c Exceed And Excel (AUS) - My Love Thomas (IRE) (Cadeaux Genereux)
084 **EJADAH** (IRE) 2 b f Clodovil (IRE) - Bintalreef (USA) (Diesis)
085 **EL NAJMM** (IRE) 2 ch c Sea The Stars (IRE) - My Dubai (IRE) (Dubai Millennium)
086 **ELSHAADIN** 2 gr f Dalakhani (IRE) - Distinctive Look (IRE) (Danehill (USA))
087 **EMARATIYA ANA** (IRE) 2 b f Excellent Art - Tina Heights (Shirley Heights)
088 **GO SAKHEE** 2 br c Sakhee's Secret - Bling Bling (IRE) (Indian Ridge)
089 **HADAATHA** (IRE) 2 gr f Sea The Stars (IRE) - Hathrah (IRE) (Linamix (FR))
090 **HERBAH** 2 b f Dansili - Khulood (USA) (Storm Cat (USA))
091 **HIGH ACCOLADE** 2 ch f Medicean - Hightime Heroine (IRE) (Danetime (IRE))
092 **HIGHLY EXCITED** (USA) 2 ch c Exchange Rate (USA) - Miss Delta Dawn (USA) (Thirty Six Red (USA))
093 **IDDER** (IRE) 2 br c Authorized (IRE) - Epiphany (Zafonic (USA))
094 **IGIDER** (IRE) 2 b c Teofilo (IRE) - Changeable (Dansili)
095 **KAFEEL** (USA) 2 b c First Samurai (USA) - Ishraak (USA) (Sahm (USA))
096 **KEEPER'S RING** (USA) 2 b f Street Cry (IRE) - Liffey Dancer (IRE) (Sadler's Wells (USA))
097 **KHATIBA** (IRE) 2 b f Kheleyf (USA) - Tempete (Dubai Millennium)
098 **LADY SPARKLER** (IRE) 2 b f Tamayuz - Capote West (USA) (Capote (USA))
099 **LAFTAH** (IRE) 2 b f Invincible Spirit (IRE) - Liscune (IRE) (King's Best (USA))
100 **MASTER OF ALKMAAR** 2 ch c Dutch Art - Lalina (GER) (Trempolino (USA))
101 **MUHAWALAH** (IRE) 2 ch f Nayef (USA) - Al Ishq (FR) (Nureyev (USA))
102 **MUNATAS** 2 b c Sea The Stars (IRE) - Dashing (IRE) (Sadler's Wells (USA))
103 **MUSHIR** 2 b c Oasis Dream - Shimah (USA) (Storm Cat (USA))

104 **MUTARAADIF** (USA) 2 b c Dynaformer (USA) - Dawla (Alhaarth (IRE))
105 **PRINCESS NOOR** (IRE) 2 b f Holy Roman Emperor (IRE) - Gentle Night (Zafonic (USA))
106 **QUASQAZAH** 2 ch c Bahamian Bounty - Rock Lily (Rock of Gibraltar (IRE))
107 **RAPID ADVANCE** 2 b c Medicean - Snow Gretel (IRE) (Green Desert (USA))
108 **SHERIFF'S STAR** (IRE) 2 gr c Lawman (FR) - Silver Bandana (USA) (Silver Buck (USA))
109 **SPIRIT OF ALSACE** (IRE) 2 b f Invincible Spirit (IRE) - Alsace (King's Best (USA))
110 **STAR JET** (IRE) 2 br gr f Teofilo (IRE) - Silver Shoon (IRE) (Fasliyev (USA))
111 **SYNERGISE** 2 ch c Danehill Dancer (IRE) - Splashdown (Falbrav (IRE))
112 **TA AMMOL** 2 b f Halling (USA) - Anaamil (IRE) (Darshaan)
113 **TEARS OF THE SUN** 2 b f Mastercraftsman (IRE) - Perfect Star (Act One)
114 **THURAYAAT** 2 b f Tamayuz - Ghaidaa (IRE) (Cape Cross (IRE))
115 **TOOFI** (FR) 2 b c Henrythenavigator (USA) - Silver Bark (Royal Applause)
116 **YAGHEER** (IRE) 2 b c Lawman (FR) - Dawn Raid (IRE) (Docksider (USA))
117 **YOUNG LEWIS** 2 ch c Compton Place - Highly Liquid (Entrepreneur)
118 unnamed 2 gr ro c Mastercraftsman (IRE) - Audacieuse (Rainbow Quest (USA))
119 unnamed 2 b c Exceed And Excel (AUS) - Gower Song (Singspiel (IRE))
120 unnamed 2 b c Dubawi (IRE) - Idonea (CAN) (Swain (IRE))
121 unnamed 2 b c Montjeu (IRE) - Madame Cerito (USA) (Diesis)
122 unnamed 2 b br c Candy Ride (ARG) - Tight Spin (USA) (Favorite Trick (USA))
123 unnamed 2 b c Cape Cross (IRE) - Whatizzit (Galileo (IRE))

Ed Vaughan

Machell Place Stables, Old Station Rd, Newmarket CB8 8DW

Tel: 01638 667411 **Fax:** 01638 667452 **Mobile:** 07799 144901

OLDER HORSES

001 **CLAPPED** 4 b g Royal Applause - Susun Kelapa (USA) (St Jovite (USA))
002 **DANCE AND DANCE** (IRE) 7 b g Royal Applause - Caldy Dancer (IRE) (Soviet Star (USA))
003 **FLAMBOROUGH BREEZE** 4 ro f Ad Valorem (USA) - Lothian Lass (IRE) (Daylami (IRE))
004 **LEGENDARY** 4 b g Exceed And Excel (AUS) - Red Carnation (IRE) (Polar Falcon (USA))
005 **REDVERS** (IRE) 5 br g Ishiguru (USA) - Cradle Brief (IRE) (Brief Truce (USA))
006 **ROBIN HOODS BAY** 5 b g Motivator - Bijou A Moi (Rainbow Quest (USA))
007 **WHITBY JET** (IRE) 5 b g Mujadil (USA) - Anazah (USA) (Diesis)

3 YEAR OLDS

008 **CLEAR PEARL** (USA) 3 ch f Giant's Causeway (USA) - Clear In The West (USA) (Gone West (USA))
009 **CLOUDWALKER** (USA) 3 b br f Tale of The Cat (USA) - Angel Flying (USA) (Saint Ballado (CAN))
010 **CROSS PATTEE** (IRE) 3 b f Oasis Dream - Victoria Cross (IRE) (Mark of Esteem (IRE))
011 **DARK TEMPLAR** 3 ch g Starcraft (NZ) - Shuaily (PER) (Shuailaan (USA))
012 **KELVINGROVE** (IRE) 3 b g Hurricane Run (IRE) - Silversword (FR) (Highest Honor (FR))
013 **KINGSTON EUCALYPT** 3 b f Halling (USA) - Derartu (AUS) (Last Tycoon)
014 **MINI BOSS** (IRE) 3 b g Street Boss (USA) - Mini Brush (USA) (Broad Brush (USA))
015 **OLIVERS MOUNT** 3 ch c Mount Nelson - Phoebe Woodstock (IRE) (Grand Lodge (USA))
016 **ON WITH THE DANCE** (IRE) 3 ch g Byron - Caldy Dancer (IRE) (Soviet Star (USA))

2 YEAR OLDS

017 **CLAIM THE ROSES** (USA) 2 b br c Speightstown (USA) - Reboot (USA) (Rubiano (USA))
018 **COSTA FILEY** 2 b c Pastoral Pursuits - Cosmic Destiny (IRE) (Soviet Star (USA))
019 **CYPRESS POINT** (FR) 2 gr f Oratorio (IRE) - Miss Sazanica (FR) (Zafonic (USA))
020 **GENUINE QUALITY** (USA) 2 b f Elusive Quality (USA) - Genuine Devotion (IRE) (Rock of Gibraltar (IRE))
021 **LADY LOVELACE** 2 b f Byron - Grain of Salt (Montjeu (IRE))
022 **PERCYS PRINCESS** 2 b f Sir Percy - Enford Princess (Pivotal)
023 **QUAINTRELLE** (IRE) 2 b f Dandy Man (IRE) - Extravagance (IRE) (King's Best (USA))
024 **REAFFIRMED** (IRE) 2 ch c Pivotal - Quiet Protest (USA) (Kingmambo (USA))
025 unnamed 2 gr c Dalakhani (IRE) - Adventure (USA) (Unbridled's Song (USA))
026 unnamed 2 b c Authorized (IRE) - Eternity Ring (Alzao (USA))
027 unnamed 2 ch c Mount Nelson - Lacework (Pivotal)
028 unnamed 2 b br c Rock Hard Ten (USA) - To The Brim (CAN) (Ascot Knight (CAN))
029 unnamed 2 ch g Bertolini (USA) - Welcome Star (IRE) (Most Welcome)

Mrs Lucy Wadham

The Trainer's House, Moulton Paddocks, Newmarket, Suffolk CB8 7PJ

Tel: 01638 662411 **Fax:** 01638 668821 **Mobile:** 07980 545776

OLDER HORSES

001 **ALL ANNALENA** (IRE) 7 b m Dubai Destination (USA) - Alla Prima (IRE) (In The Wings)
002 **AVIADOR** (GER) 7 b g Paolini (Ger) - Albarana (GER) (Sure Blade (USA))
003 **BABYSHINE** (IRE) 7 b m King's Theatre (IRE) - Brambleshine (IRE) (Phardante (FR))
004 **BOLIVIA** (GER) 7 ch m Monsun (GER) - Be My Lady (GER) (Be My Guest (USA))
005 **BRUNTON BLUE** 8 b m Compton Place - Persian Blue (Persian Bold)
006 **CANUSPOTIT** 6 b g Nomadic Way (USA) - Play Alone (IRE) (Mandalus)
007 **DALIANCE** (IRE) 4 ch g Dalakhani (IRE) - Everlasting Love (Pursuit of Love)
008 **DAWN TWISTER** (GER) 6 br g Monsun (GER) - DawnSide (CAN) (Bold Forbes)
009 **ELEAZAR** (GER) 12 b br g Alkalde (GER) - Eicidora (GER) (Surumu (GER))
010 **HORTENSE MANCINI** 4 ch f King's Best (USA) - Have Fun (Indian Ridge)
011 **LANCEUR** (FR) 4 b g Rail Link - Lanciana (IRE) (Acatenango (GER))
012 **LE REVE** (IRE) 5 br g Milan - Open Cry (IRE) (Montelimar (USA))
013 **MANSHOOR** (IRE) 8 gr g Linamix (FR) - Lady Wells (IRE) (Sadler's Wells (USA))
014 **MIDNIGHT MACARENA** 8 ch m Midnight Legend - Royal Tango (Petoski)
015 **MINSTREL'S GALLERY** (IRE) (4 ch g Refuse To Bend (IRE) - Lilakiya (IRE) (Dr Fong (USA))
016 **MISTRAL REINE** 4 b f King's Theatre (IRE) - Classic Gale (USA) (Classic Cliche (IRE))
017 **NOBLE SILK** 4 gr g Sir Percy - Tussah (Daylami (IRE))
018 **OPUS** (IRE) 4 br g Danehill Dancer (IRE) - Mixed Blessing (Lujain (USA))
019 **PERFORCE** 4 b g Sir Percy - Enforce (USA) (Kalanisi (IRE)
020 **QUEEN AVALON** 4 b f Overbury (IRE) - Newton Mo (Homo Sapien)
021 **RASHEED** 5 b g Oasis Dream - Alexandrine (IRE) (Nashwan (USA))
022 **RISING TEAL** 4 b f Phoenix Reach (IRE) - Tealby (Efisio)
023 **ROAD TO FREEDOM** 4 b g Revoque (IRE) - Go Classic (Classic Cliche (IRE))
024 **SONGSMITH** 5 b g Librettist (USA) - Venus Rising (Observatory (USA))
025 **TEALISSIO** 7 b g Helissio (FR) - Tealby (Efisio)
026 **THE BLACK BARON** (IRE) 11 br g Lord Americo - Royal Nora (IRE) (Dromod Hill)
027 **TUSCANIA** 5 b m King's Best (USA) - Contiguous (USA) (Danzig (USA))
028 **WATERED SILK** 5 gr g Encosta De Lago (AUS) - Tussah (Daylami (IRE)
029 **WIESENTRAUM** (GER) 7 ch g Next Desert (IRE) - Wiesenblute (GER) (Big Shuffle (USA))

3 YEAR OLDS

030 **ALIZEE JAVILEX** (FR) 3 b f Le Fou (IRE) - Etoile du Lion (FR) (New Target (IRE))
031 **NULLARBOR SKY** (IRE) 3 gr f Aussie Rules (USA) - Grenouillere (USA) (Alysheba (USA))
032 **PERNICA** 3 b f Sir Percy - Nicola Bella (IRE) (Sadler's Wells (USA))
033 **ZIGGY'S SECRET** 3 b f Sakhee's Secret - Ziggy Zaggy (Diktat)
034 unnamed 3 br f Notnowcato - Arruhan (IRE) (Mujtahid (USA))

2 YEAR OLDS

035 **BARI** (IRE) 2 b f Cape Cross (IRE) - Genoa (Zafonic (USA))
036 **LADY TIANA** 2 b f Sir Percy - Cartoon (Danehill Dancer (IRE))
037 **MARY LE BOW** 2 b f Sir Percy - Bermondsey Girl (Bertolini (USA))

Ed Walker

Grange House Stables, Hamilton Road, Newmarket, CB8 0TE

Tel: 01638 730710 **Mobile:** 07787 534145

OLDER HORSES

001 **ANYA** 4 b f Monsieur Bond (IRE) - Dyanita (Singspiel (IRE))
002 **AXIOM** 9 ch g Pivotal - Exhibitor (USA) (Royal Academy (USA))
003 **CATERINA DE MEDICI** (FR) 4 b f Redoute's Choice (AUS) - Night Dhu (Montjeu (IRE))
004 **DANNIOS** 7 b g Tobougg (IRE) - Fleuve d'Or (IRE) (Last Tycoon)
005 **DUKE OF DESTINY** (IRE) 4 br g Bachelor Duke (USA) - Marghelan (FR) (Soviet Star (USA))
006 **HIGH NET WORTH** 4 b g Oasis Dream - Return (USA) (Sadler's Wells (USA))
007 **INDIAN JACK** (IRE) 5 ch g Indian Haven - Almaviva (IRE) (Grand Lodge (USA))
008 **LIVIA'S DREAM** (IRE) 4 b f Teofilo (IRE) - Brindisi (Dr Fong (USA))
009 **NICHOLASCOPERNICUS** (IRE) 4 ch g Medicean - Ascendancy (Sadler's Wells (USA))
010 **RUSCELLO** (IRE) 4 b g Cape Cross (IRE) - Sea Picture (IRE) (Royal Academy (USA))
011 **WILLIE WAG TAIL** (USA) 4 b g Theatrical - Night Risk (USA) (Wild Again (USA))

3 YEAR OLDS

012 **ABLE DASH** 3 ch g Dutch Art - Evasive Quality (FR) (Highest Honor (FR))
013 **CARNEADES** (IRE) 3 b g Exceed And Excel (AUS) - Ivy League Star (IRE) (Sadler's Wells (USA))
014 **DARING DRAGON** 3 gr g Intikhab (USA) - The Manx Touch (IRE) (Petardia)
015 **GLORIOUS PROTECTOR** (IRE) 3 b c Azamour (IRE) - Hasaiyda (IRE) (Hector Protector (USA))
016 **GLORIOUS STAR** (IRE) 3 ch g Soviet Star (USA) - Caerlonore (IRE) (Traditionally (USA))
017 **INDIAN TRIFONE** (IRE) 3 ch c Indian Haven - Almaviva (IRE) (Grand Lodge (USA))
018 **SAN GABRIEL** (IRE) 3 b c Soviet Star (USA) - Rancho Cucamonga (IRE) (Raphane (USA))
019 **SCARLET ROSEFINCH** 3 ch f Cockney Rebel (IRE) - Fur Will Fly (Petong)
020 **SOUND OF GUNS** 3 b f Acclamation - Eastern Lily (USA) (Eastern Echo (USA))
021 **SURGE AHEAD** (IRE) 3 b c Danehill Dancer (IRE) - Croisiere (USA) (Capote (USA))
022 **YOU'RE THE BOSS** 3 b c Royal Applause - Trinny (Rainbow Quest (USA))

2 YEAR OLDS

023 **AYA'S GIFT** 2 ch c Compton Place - Ringarooma (Erhaab (USA))
024 **BEASTFROMTHEEAST** 2 b g Oratorio (IRE) - Bronze Star (Mark of Esteem (IRE))
025 **BUSHCRAFT** (IRE) 2 b c Bushranger (IRE) - Lady Lucia (IRE) (Royal Applause)
026 **CENSORIUS** 2 b c Notnowcato - Meredith (Medicean)
027 **CHUCK HATCH** 2 b c Sakhee (USA) - Forest Fire (SWE) (Never So Bold)
028 **CLEAR SPELL** (IRE) 2 b c Tamayuz - Beat The Rain (Beat Hollow)
029 **FRESH KINGDOM** (IRE) 2 ch g Dubawi (IRE) - Polyquest (IRE) (Poliglote)
030 **FULL MOON FEVER** (IRE) 2 b f Azamour (IRE) - Hasaiyda (IRE) (Hector Protector (USA))
031 **GLORIOUS EMPIRE** (IRE) 2 br c Holy Roman Emperor (IRE) - Humble And Proud (IRE) (Pivotal)
032 **GLORIOUS SUN** 2 b c Medicean - Sweet Cando (IRE) (Royal Applause)
033 **GRACEFILLY** 2 b f Invincible Spirit (IRE) - Marula (IRE) (Sadler's Wells (USA))
034 **HOPEFILLY** (IRE) 2 b f Compton Place - Kondakova (IRE) (Soviet Star (USA))
035 **INCREDIBLE FRESH** (IRE) 2 b c Bushranger (IRE) - Red Fox (IRE) (Spectrum (IRE))
036 **INVINCIBLE FRESH** (IRE) 2 b c Footstepsinthesand - Princess Serena (USA) (Unbridled's Song (USA))
037 **MOUTAI** 2 b c Royal Applause - Naizak (Medicean)
038 **OUTLAWED** 2 b c Kyllachy - Regent's Park (Green Desert (USA))
039 **PERSONA GRATA** 2 b f Sir Percy - Kaldounya (Kaldoun (FR))
040 **PHANTOM SPIRIT** 2 b f Invincible Spirit (IRE) - Jackie's Opera (FR) (Indian Ridge)
041 **TWENTY ROSES** (IRE) 2 b f Mastercraftsman (IRE) - Stunning Rose (IRE) (Sadler's Wells (USA))
042 **URBAN SANCTUARY** 2 ch c Mount Nelson - White Dress (IRE) (Pivotal)
043 **VEYA** (USA) 2 ch c Giant's Causeway (USA) - Gossamer (USA) (Seattle Slew (USA))
044 **XANTHOS** 2 ch g Medicean - My Girl Jode (Haafhd)

045 unnamed 2 gr f Mastercraftsman (IRE) - Amathia (IRE) (Darshaan)
046 unnamed 2 b c Notnowcato - Blaenavon (Cadeaux Genereux)
047 unnamed 2 b c Shamardal (USA) - Catch The Moon (IRE) (Peintre Celebre (USA))
048 unnamed 2 b f Acclamation - Divert (IRE) (Averti (IRE))
049 unnamed 2 b f Bahamian Bounty - Loveleaves (Polar Falcon (USA))
050 unnamed 2 b c Myboycharlie (IRE) - Madam President (Royal Applause)
051 unnamed 2 b f Invincible Spirit (IRE) - Madura (GER) (Dashing Blade)
052 unnamed 2 b c Pastoral Pursuits - Messelina (Noverre (USA))
053 unnamed 2 b c Selkirk (USA) - Starlit Sands (Oasis Dream)
054 unnamed 2 ch c Dutch Art - Stravie (IRE) (Stravinsky (USA))
055 unnamed 2 b f Compton Place - Vellena (Lucky Story (USA))

Chris Wall

Induna Stables, Fordham Road, Newmarket, Suffolk CB8 7AQ

Tel: (Home) 01638 668896 **Fax:** 01638 667279 **Mobile:** 07764 940255

OLDER HORSES

001 **BASSARA** (IRE) 4 b f Oasis Dream - Sauvage (FR) (Sri Pekan (USA))
002 **CURLY COME HOME** 4 b f Notnowcato - Cuyamaca (IRE) (Desert King (IRE))
003 **INTENSE PINK** 4 b f Pivotal - Clincher Club (Polish Patriot (USA))
004 **LANGHAM LILY** (USA) 4 b br f Badge of Silver (USA) - Silver Frau (USA) (Silver Charm (USA))
005 **NO JUSTICE** 5 b g Authorized (IRE) - Regrette Rien (USA) (Unbridled's Song (USA))
006 **OH SO SPICY** 6 ch m Pastoral Pursuits - Almasi (IRE) (Petorius)
007 **PEARL BLUE** (IRE) 5 b m Exceed And Excel (AUS) - Sanfrancullinan (IRE) (Bluebird (USA))
008 **PREMIO LOCO** (USA) 9 ch g Prized (USA) - Crazee Mental (Magic Ring (IRE))
009 **QANAN** 4 b g Green Desert (USA) - Strings (Unfuwain (USA))
010 **ROYAL ROCK** 9 b g Sakhee (USA) - Vanishing Point (USA) (Caller I D (USA))
011 **SNOW HILL** 5 gr g Halling (USA) - Swift Dispersal (Shareef Dancer (USA))

3 YEAR OLDS

012 **BALLYSHONAGH** 3 b f Tiger Hill (IRE) - Shamara (IRE) (Spectrum (IRE))
013 **BLESSING BOX** 3 b f Bahamian Bounty - Bible Box (IRE) (Bin Ajwaad (IRE))
014 **EMERALD SEA** 3 b f Green Desert (USA) - Wind Surf (USA) (Lil's Lad (USA))
015 **FIRST PENINSULAR** 3 ch c Excellent Art - Sarah's First (Cadeaux Genereux)
016 **GOOD AS NEW** 3 b f Araafa (IRE) - New Design (IRE) (Bluebird (USA))
017 **GRAVITATIONAL** (IRE) 3 b g Invincible Spirit (IRE) - Flower of Kent (USA) (Diesis)
018 **MEET ME HALFWAY** 3 b f Exceed And Excel (AUS) - Pivotal Drive (IRE) (Pivotal)
019 **NEVER TOO MUCH** (IRE) 3 b g Johannesburg (USA) - Muskoka Dawn (USA) (Miswaki (USA))
020 **OH SO SASSY** 3 b f Pastoral Pursuits - Almasi (IRE) (Petorius)
021 **PEARL QUEEN** (USA) 3 b br f Street Sense (USA) - Island Queen (USA) (Ogygian (USA))
022 **POSH BOY** (IRE) 3 b g Duke of Marmalade (IRE) - Sauvage (FR) (Sri Pekan (USA))
023 **RAINBOWS AND ROSES** 3 ch f Beat Hollow - Rainbow Sky (Rainbow Quest (USA))
024 **RAVENSBURG** 3 ch f Raven's Pass (USA) - Generous Lady (Generous (IRE))
025 **ROCKSILLA** 3 b f Rock of Gibraltar (IRE) - Hope Island (IRE) (Titus Livius (FR))
026 **RUNNINGLIKETHEWIND** (IRE) 3 b g Hurricane Run (IRE) - Virgin Hawk (USA) (Silver Hawk (USA))
027 **SILVALA DANCE** 3 b f Kyllachy - Bride of The Sea (Cape Cross (IRE))
028 **SMART ALICE** 3 b f Soviet Star (USA) - Ailincala (IRE) (Pursuit of Love)
029 **SWITCH ON** 3 b c Oasis Dream - Noodle Soup (USA) (Alphabet Soup (USA))
030 **THOUSAND KISSES** 3 b f Authorized (IRE) - Trinkila (USA) (Cat Thief (USA))
031 **TIGER JIM** 3 b g Tiger Hill (IRE) - Quintrell (Royal Applause)
032 **TRUCANINI** 3 b f Mount Nelson - Jalissa (Mister Baileys)
033 **VANDROSS** (IRE) 3 b g Iffraaj - Mrs Kanning (Distant View (USA))

2 YEAR OLDS

034 **BURMESE BREEZE** 2 b g Shirocco (GER) - Crimson Topaz (Hernando (FR))
035 **DISTANT SHADOW** 2 gr f Rock of Gibraltar (IRE) - Daheeya (Daylami (IRE))
036 **ELEUSIS** 2 b f Elnadim (USA) - Demeter (USA) (Diesis)
037 **JOHARA** (IRE) 2 b f Iffraaj - Hurricane Irene (IRE) (Green Desert (USA))
038 **MAY QUEEN** 2 ch f Shamardal (USA) - Mango Lady (Dalakhani (IRE))
039 **MR WIN** (IRE) 2 b c Intikhab (USA) - Midnight Oasis (Oasis Dream)
040 **SYRIAN PEARL** 2 gr f Clodovil (IRE) - Syrian Queen (Slip Anchor)
041 **THE NEW PHARAOH** (IRE) 2 b c Montjeu (IRE) - Out West (USA) (Gone West (USA))
042 unnamed 2 b c Teofilo (IRE) - Kalagold (IRE) (Magical Strike (USA))

Miss Amy Weaver

Rear Yard, The Severals, Newmarket CB8 7BS
Correspondence to 19 Millbank, Newmarket CB8 0EQ

Mobile: 07947 442083

OLDER HORSES

001 **CARINYA** (IRE) 5 br m Iffraaj - Ma N'Ieme Biche (USA) (Key To The Kingdom (USA))
002 **EMKANAAT** 5 b g Green Desert (USA) - Miss Anabaa (Anabaa (USA))
003 **FLORALYS** (USA) 4 b f Flower Alley (USA) - Search Mission (USA) (Red Ransom (USA))
004 **NORTH STAR BOY** (IRE) 4 b g Acclamation - Isla Azul (IRE) (Machiavellian (USA))
005 **TARIQ TOO** 6 ch g Kyllachy - Tatora (Selkirk (USA))

2 YEAR OLDS

006 unnamed 2 gr c Clodovil (IRE) - Ardesia Si (FR) (Treasure Kay)
007 unnamed 2 b g War Chant (USA) - One Frisky Cat (CAN) (Tale of The Cat (USA))
008 unnamed 2 b c Royal Applause - Prowse (USA) (King of Kings (IRE))
009 unnamed 2 ch c Dandy Man (IRE) - Sharp Diversion (USA) (Diesis)

Michael Wigham

Hamilton Stables, Hamilton Road, Newmarket, Suffolk CB8 7JQ

Tel: 01638 668806 **Fax:** 01638 668806 **Mobile:** 07831 456426

NO HORSE LIST AVAILABLE AT TIME OF GOING TO PRESS

Stuart C Williams

Diomed Stables, Hamilton Road, Newmarket CB8 0PD

Tel: (Home and **Fax**) 01638 560143 Mobile: 07730 314102

OLDER HORSES

001 **AQUILONIUS** (IRE) 4 b c Soviet Star (USA) - Via Verbano (IRE) (Caerleon (USA))
002 **BLUE JACK** 8 b g Cadeaux Genereux - Fairy Flight (IRE) (Fairy King (USA))
003 **CHAPTER SEVEN** 4 ch g Excellent Art - My First Romance (Danehill (USA))
004 **CINCINNATI KIT** 4 br f Cape Cross (IRE) - Princess Georgina (Royal Applause)
005 **DOCTOR PARKES** 7 b g Diktat - Lucky Parkes (Full Extent (USA))
006 **ETON RIFLES** (IRE) 8 b g Pivotal - Maritsa (IRE) (Danehill (USA))
007 **EX ORIENTE** (IRE) 4 b g Azamour (IRE) - Little Whisper (IRE) (Be My Guest (USA))
008 **MY KINGDOM** (IRE) 7 b g King's Best (USA) - Nebraas (Green Desert (USA))
009 **PETTOCHSIDE** 4 b g Refuse To Bend (IRE) - Clear Impression (IRE) (Danehill (USA))
010 **PRINCELY SUM** (IRE) 4 b g Refuse To Bend (IRE) - Green Dollar (IRE) (Kingmambo (USA))
011 **RESONARE** 4 b g Echo of Light - Pretty Kool (Inchinor)
012 **SIM SALA BIM** 5 gr ro h Act One - Francia (Legend of France (USA))
013 **TAROOQ** (USA) 7 b g War Chant (USA) - Rose of Zollern (IRE) (Seattle Dancer (USA))
014 **THE STRIG** 6 b g Mujahid (USA) - Pretty Kool (Inchinor)
015 **WELEASE BWIAN** (IRE) 4 b g Kheleyf (USA) - Urbanize (USA) (Chester House (USA))

3 YEAR OLDS

016 **BAHAMA BAY** 3 b f Bahamian Bounty - Green Bonnet (IRE) (Green Desert (USA))
017 **CHARLOTTE RHODES** 3 b f Halling (USA) - Kunda (IRE) (Intikhab (USA))
018 **CHERRY PRINCESS** 3 ch gr f Act One - Francia (Legend of France (USA))
019 **HELAMIS** 3 b f Shirocco (GER) - Alnoor (USA) (Danzig (USA))
020 **HOLLEY SHIFTWELL** 3 ch f Bahamian Bounty - Persario (Bishop of Cashel)
021 **LADY GUINEVERE** 3 b f Pivotal - Birdie (Alhaarth (IRE))
022 **LITTLE ALICE** 3 ch f Haafhd - Allespagne (USA) (Trempolino (USA))
023 **MILL I AM** (USA) 3 b f Henny Hughes (USA) - Courageous (USA) (Kingmambo (USA))
024 **TOP BANANA** 3 b g Tiger Hill (IRE) - Special Green (FR) (Sadler's Wells (USA))
025 **TYCHAIOS** 3 b g Green Desert (USA) - Tychy (Suave Dancer (USA))
026 **WELSH MOONLIGHT** 3 ch f Vita Rosa (JPN) - Moonlight Applause (Royal Applause)

2 YEAR OLDS

027 **CHAINSAW** 2 b c Pastoral Pursuits - Roodeye (Inchinor)
028 **DODGER MARLEY** (IRE) 2 b c Kodiac - Shelini (Robellino (USA))
029 **DRINKUPTRIG** (IRE) 2 b c Bushranger (IRE) - Maybe in May (USA) (Miswaki (USA))
030 **FREDERIC CHOPIN** 2 ch c Tamayuz - Eliza Gilbert (Noverre (USA))
031 **GLOBAL EXPLORER** (USA) 2 b c Henrythenavigator (USA) - Trulips (USA) (Elusive Quality (USA))
032 **NOVA CHAMP** (IRE) 2 ch c Intikhab (USA) - Baby Bunting (Wolfhound (USA))
033 **STAPLEFORD** LAD 2 b c Shirocco (GER) - World Spirit (Agnes World (USA))
034 **SYBILICIOUS** 2 b f Royal Applause - Tora Bora (Grand Lodge (USA))
035 **TETE ORANGE** 2 ch f Pastoral Pursuits - Imperialistic (IRE) (Imperial Ballet (IRE))
036 **WIKI TIKI** 2 br f Dixie Union (USA) - Witten (USA) (Fusaichi Pegasus (USA))
037 unnamed 2 b br c War Chant (USA) - Cotton Club Ballet (USA) (Street Cry (IRE))
038 unnamed 2 b br c Artie Schiller (USA) - Ethyl Mae (USA) (Woodman (USA))
039 unnamed 2 b c Footstepsinthesand - Gold Marie (IRE) (Green Desert (USA))
040 unnamed 2 b c Cape Cross (IRE) - Muluk (IRE) (Rainbow Quest (USA))

TRAINING GALLOPS AT NEWMARKET

RACECOURSE SIDE – GALLOPS AND CANTERS - 2013

TURF GALLOP/CANTER	OPENS	CLOSES	MAXIMUM DISTANCE
July Canter	when Flat Season starts	end of Flat Season	7f
Peat Moss Between the Banks	drought conditions		7f
Peat Moss Gallop	drought conditions		2m
Summer Gallop	dry conditions		2m
Summer Canter	in conjunction with Summer Gallop, in dry conditions		6-7f
Watered Gallop	on applications and in drought conditions – Tuesday, Wednesday, Friday & Saturday only	1030	9f
Back of the Flat Gallop	5 weeks before start of Flat Turf Season	when Flat Gallop opens	1m 4f
Back of the Flat Canter	when Flat Gallop opens	end of Flat Turf Season	1m 4f
The Flat Gallop	3 weeks before start of Flat Turf Season	end of Flat Turf Season	1m 6f
Southfields	after Flat Turf Season	middle of April (may close earlier if ground used up)	1m 4f
Southfields – Yearlings	after Flat Turf Season	middle of April (may close earlier if ground used up)	7f

Southfields New Winter Ground up and down Canter	after Flat Turf Season (if ground conditions are suitable)	middle of May (may close earlier if ground is used up)	6f up 7f down
Short Canter by side of Rowley Mile road	Newmarket racedays and Saturdays during the Flat Season		4f
Choke Jade Canter	1 February (if ground conditions are suitable)	end of February	5-6f

ARTIFICIAL GALLOP/CANTER	**OPENS**	**CLOSES FOR MAINTENANCE**	**MAXIMUM DISTANCE**
Cambridge Road (Polytrack)	general work throughout the year	0800-0830 daily 1000-1030 if needed	1m 3f
Hamilton Hill (Polytrack)	general work throughout the year	0800-0815 daily 1015-1030 daily	4½f
Links Away Canter (Cushion Track)	open all year	when needed	4f
Rowley Mile Away Canter (Ecotrack)	open all year	when needed	6f
Rubbing House (Polytrack)	general work throughout the year	0930-1000 daily	9f
Southfields Wood Chip Canter	general work throughout the year	0930-1000	7f
Southfields Round Canter (Ecotrack)	open all year right-handed until 0900 left-handed after 0920	0900-0920 daily	6f

TRAINING GALLOPS AT NEWMARKET

BURY SIDE – GALLOPS AND CANTERS - 2013

TURF GALLOP/CANTER	OPENS	CLOSES	MAXIMUM DISTANCE
Warren Hill Canter	1 February (if ground conditions are suitable)	middle of May	4f
Side Hill Canter	open all year (if ground conditions are suitable)		1m 4f
Bury Hill Canter	middle of May (if ground conditions are suitable)	end of Flat Turf Season	1m
Long Hill Gallop	middle of May (closes when the Limekilns Canter is open)	when Peat Moss Gallop opens on Limekilns	1m
Long Hill Canter	middle of May (if ground conditions are suitable)	end of Flat Turf Season	1m
Centres of New Ground, Bury Hill, Private Ground – yearlings only	1 November (if ground conditions are suitable)	1 March	
Waterhall: Middle Canter	25 January (if ground conditions are suitable)	middle of May	7f
Waterhall: Line Gallop	5 clear Saturdays before start of Flat Turf Season	middle of May	9f
Waterhall: Special Gallop	on application		6½f
Waterhall – National Hunt horses only	November	middle of March	1m+
LIMEKILNS Short Gallop	dry conditions		1m
Long Gallop (Peat Moss)	drought conditions		1m+

Canter	dry conditions		1m
Round Gallop	on application in drought conditions		1m 2f
Golden Mile (Trial Ground)	on application in drought conditions		1m
Railway Land Canter	open all year		4-5f
Private Ground Peat Moss Canter	dry conditions opens with Short Gallop on Limekilns		9f

ARTIFICIAL GALLOP/CANTER	OPENS	CLOSES FOR MAINTENANCE	MAXIMUM DISTANCE
Al Bahathri Polytrack	open throughout the year galloping only until 7.50 am	0750-0810 if needed 0900-0920 daily 1020-1040 if needed	9f
Bury Hill Ecotrack	general work throughout the year	0840-0900 daily 1015-1035 daily	1m 2f
Long Hill Polytrack	general work throughout the year	0815-0830 daily 0950-1005 daily	7½f
Railway Land Protrack Down Canter	open all year	when needed	7f
Side Hill Polytrack	general work throughout the year	0830-0900 if needed	1m 2f
Town Canter Ecotrack	general work throughout the year	0800-0810 daily 0935-0945 daily	5f
Warren Hill Polytrack	general work throughout the year	when needed	4f
Warren Hill MacTrac	general work throughout the year	when needed	4f

Silverfeet®

Barrier Protection and Hoof Balm for Daily Use

www.silverfeet.co.uk

Farriers and horse owners turn their attention to a new daily use hoof care product designed and manufactured in the UK.

In 2010, two fathers were watching their children showjumping when one asked the other whether he knew of an additive that would render hoof oil antimicrobial. The two Dads were John Stanley, a Master Farrier with 22 years experience and Dr Richard Hixson, a Consultant Anaesthetist who had an interest in antimicrobial coatings. John had witnessed firsthand the detrimental effects of hoof infections and wanted to offer his clients a product that would prevent problems occurring. The discussion continued for some months and, after a period of research, development and experimentation with manufacturing methods, Silverfeet Hoof Balm was created.

The team ultimately decided on a natural oil/beeswax base combined with a medical-grade silver complex. Laboratory and field tests showed these constituents, when combined through a patent-pending manufacturing method, produced a balm that did not freeze or melt at extremes of temperature, was safe to apply to the wall, sole and frog on a daily basis and yet was highly effective in reducing bacterial contamination within just a few hours of application.

To successfully incorporate silver into the base ingredients was a crucial step in the development process. Although a number of heavy metals are known to be antimicrobial, they are either too expensive, too toxic or are required in concentrations too high to be of practical use. The antimicrobial properties of silver have been utilised for thousands of years and fortunately this effect is exhibited in a very low, safe concentration.

"Silver really is an excellent choice for our product" says Richard Hixson. "It prevents bacteria growing, disrupts their energy supply and stops them reproducing. Unlike antibiotics, resistance does not occur and unlike harsh chemicals, it is safe for use as prevention. The silver incorporated in Silverfeet is exactly the same as found in medical equipment and countless other commercially available products; even socks and riding hats."

Through careful selection of constituents, Silverfeet is manufactured free from all prohibited substances listed in current FEI publications and complies with the Rules of Racing. The balm works by creating an effective barrier against the environment whilst the beeswax maintains the silver in close contact with the hoof surface, reducing contamination and promoting healthy development.

"The laboratory results were amazing" says John Stanley, "but the most important test was always going to be the response of horse owners and farriers. The feedback however has been fantastic with regular use resulting in healthier hooves, less odour, less tenderness and in some cases, shoes staying on for longer when previously they were regularly lost. If I have one complaint, it would be that I find myself blunting my knife more frequently as the hooves are just so healthy and strong."

Silverfeet is available in four colours: natural, girly pink, boys' blue and black; designed to encourage children to participate in hoof care. Although the colours do not alter but enhance natural hoof appearance and produce a lasting shine, the Silverfeet Team were concerned they would be misinterpreted and viewed only as a gimmick. They felt however that it was essential to engage with children and encourage them to care for their ponies' feet and, with the pink and blue selling so well, the team believe they have achieved their goal in this respect.

"Although primarily endorsed by showjumpers and eventers such as Michael Whitaker, Rolf-Göran Bengtsson and Nicola Wison", says Rob Fawcett, Business Director, "there is simply no reason why Silverfeet cannot be used across all disciplines including racing. It will certainly be interesting to see whether the reported benefits result in improved racing performance. In addition, Silverfeet is designed and manufactured in Britain and it's great to introduce such a fantastic product into the UK market at this time."

"The number of farriers using and recommending Silverfeet is increasing rapidly," says John, "and we believe this is due to them seeing the benefits first hand. Silverfeet prevents problems occurring and is cost-effective compared with expensive and time-consuming treatment options. We were keen to develop the Silverfeet-Farrier relationship and so elected to sponsor both the England Farrier and Apprentice Farrier Teams at a very early stage. This has certainly been an extremely positive experience for us as a new company."

With an established UK market, The Team are now looking to expand their operations to the EU, North America and the Middle East. "Our goal is to support all owners in maintaining their horse's feet in the best possible condition" says the Team. "We have many caring owners and talented farriers in the UK and Silverfeet now provides both these groups with an effective hoof care product that truly works."

Silverfeet is available in 400 ml jars, 2.5 and 5 litre tubs can be purchased from:

Simon Curtis FWCF HonAssocRCVS,

O.A. Curtis and Sons

The Forge, Moulton Road, Newmarket, Suffolk CB8 8DU

+44 (0) 1638 665761

www.curtisfarrier.com HS-Silver Ltd.

www.silverfeet.co.uk

YOUR HORSE´S DIET? - AN INDEPENDENT SECOND OPINION IS AT HAND.

It's easy to agree that well balanced rations, based on high quality roughage, concentrates and supplements will make our horses perform better and live longer.

Getting advice from our feed supplier is certainly a good idea since their advice is generally based on scientific facts and long experience. Some of their nutritionists also use computer programs to create optimized rations for thoroughbreds and other demanding breeds. In fact, some of those same leading UK helpdesks are already using our Scandinavian software – the top-end PC-Horse Consultant version - to develop rations for their clients. PC-Horse programs provide expert advice to bring you safely into the mainstream of the equine nutrition knowledge revolution.

Developers: Knut Hove. Veterinarian and professor in animal physiology and Dag Austbø. Professor in animal nutrition with horses as a speciality.

Based on up-to-date science, all our versions use unique algorithms to make official and proven nutritional data from the UK clear and understandable. Smart functions give you advice where and when you need it.

Do you breed horses? If you do, then you know how many differences there are between horses when young. One will have strong muscles and tendons and a well-developed skeleton, while another seems to lack key features critical for optimal development. The same goes for mares as well. As a breeder, you'll know that the feeding and environment you provide is more than half the secret of success.

Are you a trainer? If so, you'll need your valuable horses to be performing at their best in a range of different circumstances. Of course all horses should not have the same feeds just because they are housed the same stable. PC-Horse helps you meet the full range and diversity of nutrition needed by the individual athletes in your stable!

An independent opinion PC-Horse enables you to obtain your own second opinion concerning feeds and nutrition – and in minutes! It comes with a range of British standard feeds, so that the values in your diets are always correct. You can also quickly formulate your own feeds using fresh feed analysis data and pre-built feed templates.

INDEX TO ADVERTISERS